Acknowledgements

In memory of Eric Costello.

"I get by with a little help from my friends..."

This book was encouraged and made possible by a little help from many of my kind friends:

Sean Cliver, Johnny "Mojo" Munnerlyn, Rhyn Noll, Rich Novak, Holly Anderson, Dave Freil, Tim Steenstra, Spyhill Skates, Mike McCarthy, Matt French, Chicken Deck, Chris Kong, Linton Kwok, Mark and Carl Bjorlund, Super Rat, Stuttgart Skate Museum, David Lamar Sultzer, Big John Evenson, Jim Raun-Byberg, Rob Roskopp, Richard Metiver, Pat O'Neill, Corey Wells, Brian Caldwell, Matt Weinstein, Andre Fernandez, Zack Garcia, Danny Keith, Santa Cruz Skateshop, Bill Ackerman, Bill's Wheels, Skateworks, Mike "Smiley" Goldman, Keith Meek, Jeff Kendall, Gavin O'Brien, Claus Grabke, Steve Alba, Ed Riggins, Skip Engblom, Christian Hosoi, Steve Olson, Natas Kaupus, Jason Jessee, Spidey Demontrond, John Hutson, Henry Hester, Tim Piumarta, Bob Denike, Richard Latorraca, Steve Keenan, Dave McIntyre, Barry Ascher, John Krisic, Russ Calish, Mickey Munoz, Bill Dawson, Kobe Yamauchi, Michio Degawa, Jiro Hanaue, Tadayuki Kato, Yuji Ikeda, Kim Ito, Rin Tanaka, Tomonori "Rip" Tanaka, Scatterbrain, the Franklins, Natal, Makoto Nakashima, Michael Brooke, Mike Moore, Fenton Savastino, Farid A. Abraham, Mike Horlick, Jeral Tidwell, Brian MacNeil, Estelle Brinius, Microtek, Rene Schlaepfer, Jeff Samuels, Dave's Computer, Steve Wozniak, Iver Flom, Steve Manuosos, Matt Weinstein, Bernie Powers, Richard "Fat Rich" Warwick, Chris Chicarella, Tim Ng, Will Simmons, Pete Simmons, Gary Partlow, Ernie Keller, Tony Hill, John DeFigh, Mike Leeds, Bruce Bard, Harry Conti, Leland Lane, Brian Hamilton, Keith Drennen, James Mazzeo, Neil Young, Tracy Nelson, Kenny Stocks, Robbie Davison, Cap Caouozzo, Luca Ionesco, Bruce and Erica Apana, Paul "Lousy" Hirscher, my sponsors below, and last but not least, my son Jimbo Phillips, my wife Dolly Phillips, and the wonderful family and staff at Schiffer Books Ltd, Peter, Nancy and Pete Schiffer.

Scribbles by Skaters poster for Ohio skateboard Expo, 2002.

Copyright © 2007 by Jim Phillips
Library of Congress Control Number: 2007926621

ISBN: 978-0-7643-2807-7
Printed in China
5 4 3 2

Published by Schiffer Publishing, Ltd.
4880 Lower Valley Road
Atglen, PA 19310
Phone: (610) 593-1777; Fax: (610) 593-2002
E-mail: Info@schifferbooks.com
Web: www.schifferbooks.com

For our complete selection of fine books on this and related subjects, please visit our website at www.schifferbooks.com. You may also write for a free catalog.

Schiffer Publishing's titles are available at special discounts for bulk purchases for sales promotions or premiums. Special editions, including personalized covers, corporate imprints, and excerpts, can be created in large quantities for special needs. For more information, contact the publisher.

We are always looking for people to write books on new and related subjects. If you have an idea for a book, please contact us at proposals@schifferbooks.com.

THE
SKATEBOARD ART
of
Jim Phillips

4880 Lower Valley Road, Atglen, PA 19310 USA

FOREWORD
by Johnny "Mojo" Munnerlyn

A skateboarder needs no introduction to the art of Jim Phillips. If you skate, you know his work - period. Logos he designed nearly thirty years ago are still brandished today and most of his celebrated graphics have become recognizable icons within the skate scene. You may even have a tattoo of one of his designs.

For those non-skaters out there, here is a little skate art history to get you up to speed. By the late seventies, most skateboard companies were satisfied with simply plopping a logo on a board and calling it done. Yet Jim Phillips and a handful of like-minded artists could see that the skateboard was more than just another "product". It was a blank canvas for self-expression. Jim's inventive visual imagery captured your attention, demanded your allegiance, and helped throw open the floodgates to a universe of divergent images. Today, he's recognized as one of skate art's true pioneers.

I met Jim Phillips in 1988 through my friend, Bob Denike, who worked at Santa Cruz Skateboards. Bob told me Jim was on the lookout for young artists capable of drawing skate comics for his Road Rash comic book and encouraged me to check it out. Already a fan of Jim's work, I jumped at the chance. I called Jim; he gave me the specs for the comic book and I quickly worked up a three-page story. When I had finished inking my piece, I drove over to Santa Cruz to personally drop it off at Jim's place. I remember him showing me the Road Rash cover-art he had drawn and some of the comics he was working on. Needless to say, I was awestruck. I was a young skate art wannabe meeting "The Man" himself. I was nervous and stoked at the same time, hoping Jim would like what I had drawn. When he said I had made the cut, I was overjoyed. As things turned out, my comic appeared in the one and only issue of Road Rash published. A career in comic books it did not launch, but it helped me get my foot in the door when the next opportunity rolled around.

A few months after I had done the comic for Road Rash, I heard Jim was enlarging his studio and hiring some young artists to help him out. I had recently quit a graphic design job I was unhappy with and was looking for work, so I called him up again. Jim remembered me, but was hesitant to give me an interview. I found out later that he was tired of doing interviews so he had devised an artist tryout test instead. It was a one-page sheet of instructions. The assignment was to design a skate sticker. The artwork had to say Santa Cruz Skateboards somewhere on it , and show someone skateboarding. This was my chance! I was determined to draw something so spectacular that he'd have no choice but to hire me. What I came up with looked like my take on Jim's signature "Slasher" character bursting through a circular Santa Cruz logo with flaming letters. Was it good enough? I'd given it my best shot, right down to the obsessively tight inking. There was only one way to find out. I arranged to see Jim again and show him the fruits of my labor. When I arrived at his place he immediately led me next door to show me his newly expanded Phillips Studios. What looked like an innocent little house on the outside had been transformed into some kind of an insane artist's lair.

Drawing tables had been installed along all the walls. Art supplies beckoned from custom contoured shelves. There was a photocopy machine and a light table. The kitchen sported a refrigerator plastered with skate stickers. If that wasn't enough, in one corner a real skull collection was on display. ("You need to draw a cat skull? No problem, there's one on the shelf over there.") How cool was that? Jim introduced me to his crew of artists who all gathered around as I unveiled my artwork. Jim seemed pleased with what he saw, which I took as a good sign, but I anxiously prepared for the inevitable critique. Before it could happen though someone blurted out "He can draw!" Jim agreed and that was it. I was in! I had made it! Jim said I could start right away and I never looked back.

John's tryout logo.

Working for Jim Phillips, however, was not like working at a regular job, it was a dream job. Phillips Studios was a skate artist's playground. Everywhere you looked there were skateboards, posters, sketches, stickers, skateboard wheels, ad layouts, doodles, skate magazines, and graphics in various stages of completion. It was a perfect storm of creative chaos into which Jim haphazardly tossed a gang of eight young "artists in training", all of us fueled by raw enthusiasm, a love of skating, and plenty of caffeine. If Jim was the mad scientist, we were his experiment. There was Jim's son, Jim Jr., better known as "Jimbo", who was just starting to follow in his father's footsteps artistically; Justin Forbes a born prankster bursting with natural artistic talent; Hermel Mayang, definitely the "most punk" guy there; hard working Andreas Ginghofer, who became the designated studio production artist; Keith Meek a well-known skater, who was looking to get his start in graphic design; Kevin Marburg, the quiet outsider who could draw circles around you: and Paul "Lousy" Hirscher, who provided a healthy dose of comic relief, and me.

Everyone dove in headfirst. We naturally checked out Jim's personal library of art books, magazines, and comics. Feasting our eyeballs on The Art of Rock, Famous Monsters of Filmland, Vigil Finlay's Phantasm, Zap Comix, and more. We enjoyed a steady soundtrack of Bad Religion, Misfits, Red Hot Chili Peppers, Bad Brains, and Social D blared from the studio boombox. Break-time meant a skate sesh on the curb out front, or making a "Dew Run" to the nearest market for a fresh supply of Mountain Dew. If a new skate video came out, we'd stop work for a studio viewing. In fact, everything we did was "artistic research." A few of us even made a memorable road trip to L.A. to check out an art show by Robert Williams (more "artistic research").

Through all this mayhem, Jim had us working our asses off. He was schooling us on our drawing techniques, showing us how to prepare artwork for reproduction, basically giving us a private education in skateboard art. Talk about on the job training! As our skills improved, Jim's confidence in us grew. When we were ready, he'd move us up to bigger projects with more responsibility. Ideas started bouncing off the walls - a real artistic camaraderie was forming. Soon we felt like an unstoppable force that could accomplish anything, even tackle the ever-mounting workload Jim was constantly facing. Jim assigned me some spot illustrations to start with. From there I worked my way up to doing backgrounds for some ads. Next came some hand lettering, then some wheel art and T-shirt assignments. Of course, what I really wanted to sink my teeth into was a board graphics.

John Munnerlyn talks with Keith Meek.

My opportunity finally came one day when Christian Hosoi and his father, Ivan, dropped by the studio to talk to Jim about graphics. We were all star-struck having a skate superstar in our midst. It turned out that Christian and Ivan were there to talk to Jim about a graphic for Sergie Ventura, one of the riders on the Hosoi team. I could see Ivan showing Jim some kind of a sketch on what looked like a paper napkin. After the Hosois left, Jim dropped Ivan's sketch on my drawing board and said, "How would you like to do this graphic?" I'll never forget that moment; though I eventually did several more board graphics while I worked at Phillips Studios, it's that Sergie Ventura graphic that stands out, maybe because it was my first board graphic, definitely because Jim Phillips thought I was good enough to do it.

When I look back on Phillips Studios now, I realize what a unique moment in time it was. Jim was at the right place, at the right time. Not only did he produce a body of work that has stood up over time, his legacy has continued on in the work of artists he helped to develop. To this day, most of Jim's proteges are still working in the fields of skate art, illustration, or graphic design - especially Jimbo, who carries on the Phillips family tradition.

The best way now to understand the significance of Phillips Studios is to put it in historical context. Skateboarding is different today. Back in the 1980s Jim was operating outside of the mainstream. Graphics are different today. Phillips Studios was pre-computer. We drew everything by hand. Comparing it to what's happening today makes little sense. To me, working at Phillips Studios in the '80s equates more with what it must have been like working at Roth Studios in the '60s. That's the best analogy I can make. Both were cultural phenomena that went on to influence underground art for years to come. Both were white-hot bursts of creative energy that came and went, but not before burning their influence into the eyeballs of a generation of impressionable youth. That's what Phillips Studios represents to me.

This book, for the first time, collects all of Jim Phillips' skate art in one volume chronologically. If you're a longtime skater, you'll recognize boards you may have once ridden. Graphics that stoked you out and made you want to skate in the first place appear here. If you're new to skate art, you've come to the right place. Jim's artwork will amaze and it will enlighten, and skate art today, owes a great deal of credit to one of its true originators, Jim Phillips.

John Munnerlyn went on to follow Jim Phillips as art director of Santa Cruz Skateboards from 1990 to 1999. Today he continues to do skate art for various companies, as well as exhibit his fine art. He resides in Santa Cruz, California with his wife and two daughters.

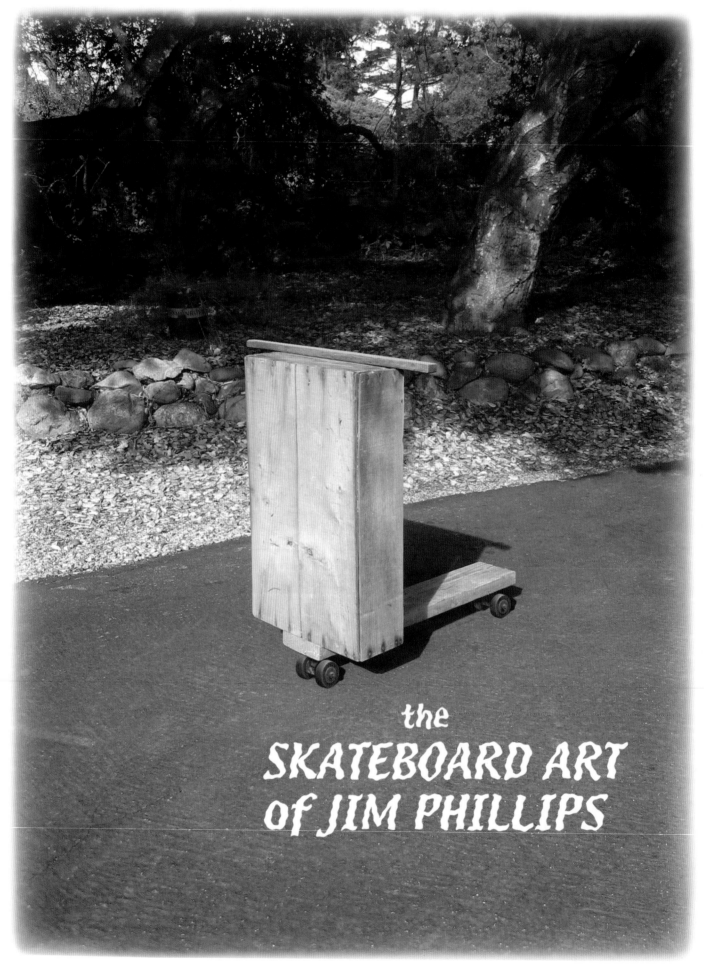

the
SKATEBOARD ART
of JIM PHILLIPS

1955

During most of 1955 I was ten years old, at least until October. My grandparents, Edna and Henry C. Hall, lived on a hillside in San Bruno, California, in an area known as South San Francisco. My parents lived in Santa Cruz, but my mother, also named Edna, often visited her mother in San Bruno. My grandparents' house on East Avenue overlooked the bay and the San Francisco Airport. You could see commercial flights taking off from the runway; that was before jet engines. Every few minutes there would be the sound of a prop engine revving up and then fading away. That was a pleasant sound to me, and it runs through my memories of the days I spent there.

With a view like that, their house was obviously built on a steep lot, as were most of the homes there. That meant hills in the neighborhood. Hills didn't mean much to me at first, except the extra effort it took to walk back from the hobby store. But that was all about to change. One day, as I was out on the sidewalk, I met a kid about my age who lived a few doors away. I think at first we just sized each other up, but I was drawn to a wooden contraption laying between us on his walkway. It was a two-by-six board with an orange crate nailed on top and metal wheels on the bottom. The crate had a stick nailed across the top, which extended about six inches on each side as handles. The wheels were obviously from a roller skate. It seemed to be a homemade four-wheel version of the two-wheel metal scooters that were built by bike companies since day one.

The kid seemed to relish my interest and said, "Go ahead, try it!" He picked up a handle and pulled the crate up on its wheels; it looked cool! He put his foot on the board, pushed with the other, and rode it towards me. He got off, offered the handle and said, "Take it down the sidewalk!" I remember his grin as I took hold of the handles and peered down the sloping sidewalk. I didn't want to seem fearful, so I said, "Sure," with faked confidence. I put my right foot on the board and gave a push with my other, like he did. The sidewalk angled at a slight decline, and it didn't take much to get it going. I stopped pushing and set my feet on the board as I rolled along with a clickety-clack sound from the sidewalk and cracks.

The feeling of motion was a rush. Vibration picked up as the speed increased. I looked back to see my new friend running far behind. I laughed and whooped out a yell, but the skate-crate started to wobble and I quickly turned to concentrate on where I was going. The sidewalk became a little steeper and I picked up speed. I discovered that leaning to the left or right would turn the path of the crate, and just on time for me to steer away from a looming telephone pole. The wind was in my face and the wheels made a grinding sound; it was intoxicating.

I tried steering, leaning this way and that, going from one side of the sidewalk to the other. I came too close to a car and pushed off its running board with my foot. I straightened out and stood up straight; I was having the time of my life. The sidewalk became steeper, and suddenly I was going

quite fast. I wanted to stop, but it dawned on me that I didn't know how that was supposed to happen. Scooters usually had a rear foot brake. I didn't have time to wonder why he forgot to mention stopping. Toward the end of the block the hill became quite steep and I was afraid to jump off. The clickety-clack and the metallic grinding sound were getting louder and vibration was growing, when the crate developed a shimmy. I tried to hold the handlebar steady but the whole contraption began to wobble. I careened toward to the foot of the hill where there was a corner at the intersection.

I knew I wouldn't be able to negotiate the corner, or even keep control, corner or not. I narrowly missed another telephone pole and in doing so leaned too far to my right. I spotted a lawn ahead on the right side, and aimed for that. As soon as the front wheels hit the grass, the crate nose-dived and I went over the box and onto the lawn. I remembered about rolling and tucked my head, and rolled across some flowers and landed on the other side.

I lay dazed, and my new friend came running up, fell on the grass and rolled around laughing. He pointed at the plowed flowers laughing, and then it struck me how funny it all was. After all, I didn't get hurt. Then I started to laugh too, and he called out, "You wanna go again?" I didn't have time to say, because suddenly a lady came out of the house brandishing a broom. We grabbed the crate and pushed it up the sidewalk as fast as we could run. After that day, I had a new friend and a lot more to look forward to when visiting the grandparents.

The skate-crate was an early form of skateboard, circa 1950s.

Bunboarding on Beach Hill, Santa Cruz, Ca. circa 1959. Pat and Mike O'Neill roll past the locals hanging out at O'Neill's Surf Shop.

1958

At home in Santa Cruz, I recalled the good times I'd had with the skate crate in San Bruno, and began looking for components to make my own. I talked my sister out of an old pair of clamp-on roller skates and nailed both halves of one to a two-by-four. You had to bend the heads over or the nail would come through the hole. I mounted a wooden box, and nailed a stick on top for the handle bar. But after I took it out front to ride, I suddenly realized how flat our street was, and with no sidewalks. As if that wasn't bad enough to quench my spirit, it was soon announced that we were moving to a new house on Marilyn Street, which turned out to be a dirt road. We moved and my dad enjoyed the low tax base. I tried to cope with my new rutted, unpaved track. It did have a slight hill, but dirt jammed my wheel bearings.

As time went by, I decided to make a skimboard. I had been spending a lot of time at the Sunny Cove and a few of the other guys had them. I managed to obtain a piece of 5/8 inch marine-grade plywood and shaped a round nose and beveled on the bottom. The tail was left square in those days, as drag to keep the nose pointed forward. After sanding, I painted it black and painted white scallops with red pinstripe around them, like I had seen on custom cars of the day. It was my first hot-rod-style art, which I would later dabble at on friends' cars. But I couldn't drive and skimboarding was free. Spring rains brought lots of new sand to the beaches. The high sand level made the waves wash across a broad stretch of sand an inch or so deep. With skimming, you run and throw your skim on the shallow water. We would jump on the board and ride all the way across the cove. It was an idyllic scene there at the Sunny Cove. I would hang out with friends from my school, which was just down the street. The unique character of the place, a deep cove about hundred and fifty feet wide, made it a fun place to swim and bodysurf the waves. Currents and rips were nonexistent because of the rock cliffs on each side. We rode waves on our tubes, and in the winter time riding waves on tubes could be hair-raising.

One of my schoolmates lived across the street from the Pleasure Point Market. He hardly ever went surfing, even though he lived across the street from the best surfing break on the coast, but he had a balsa-wood surfboard and he wanted a monster painted on the nose. Using enamels, I painted a monster face with bulging bloodshot eyes, a forked tongue, and big teeth-all contained in a circle except the tongue, which was hanging all the way out. After having my hands all over the glossy clear fiberglass and wood board for those several hours, I knew I had to have one. I went home and counted my paper route savings. In those days, there weren't any real surfboard showrooms locally. You had to ask around. Most of the surfers had boards from Southern California, with names like Velzy-Jacobs, Yater, and Hobie. I had some friends, the Rauen brothers, who said they could get me a good deal on a balsa-wood board that had been stolen from a defunct surf shop and recovered by the police. The shop was officially out of business when I went there with Dave Rauen to pick up one of the last Mako surfboards. The place looked ransacked, graffiti was on the walls, windows were broken out and trash was everywhere. I noticed a surfboard on the glassing racks that "went-off" before the rails were wrapped, and stiffly hung down. Dave said that "Murphy" the glasser was drunk. To me, it was the smell of resin that was intoxicating.

My new Mako was seventy dollars, which was my entire paper route savings. It was a "pig" model, so called because of the wide tail. Johnny Rice shaped it. The board had been scuffed-up, apparently when the thieves dragged it out of the broken windows, so Dave re-glossed the bottom in what they called an "abstract", solid orange with black streaks brushed nose to tail. It had a resined mahogany skeg, no sticker. I was elated to have my own board, and carried it down to the ocean almost every day after school. Sometimes Big John Evenson, who lived down the street, would pick me up in his woody to go surfing.

BIG JOHN EVENSON: "During that period of time I met a local surfer and artist by the name of Jimmy Phillips. We surfed almost every day, sometimes to the detriment of school. About '59, during one of the long lulls in surfing, we made a bunboard, later to be called the skateboard. Basically it was a two by four of varying lengths from two to four feet long with a skate, usually steel, which we purchased at Goodwill. We took the skate apart and nailed the front half to the front of the board and the rear nailed to the rear. Now, as with any new thing, and the surfer "go for it" attitude, we, as pioneers, pushed the envelope, always looking for steeper, longer, and faster hills."

Big John Evenson

David Lamar Sultzer

I became friends with Davey Sultzer from seeing him around the Pleasure Point neighborhood where we lived. Davey had been surfing for a while; in fact he was pretty good at it, although he was a few years younger than me. Davey had some inside track on surf culture because his mom, Marie, rented a small house in the back to Mike Winterburn, who was about the biggest local surf legend and surfboard shaper of the shaping racks set up in the carport; balsa blanks and shavings were lying around.

DAVEY SULTZER: "It's amazing how much a town can change over the years. When Jimmy and I were kids growing up in Pleasure Point, it was almost exclusively a retirement community. There were only two junior high schools and one high school in town, so there wasn't a lot of kids around. The surfing community was very small and just about everyone knew each other. I remember how Jimmy and I would ride our bikes over to old-timer Al Weimer's house on East Cliff Drive to watch him shape balsawood boards by hand in his driveway. Some of the first surf movie makers came to town and would screen their raw footage in some surfer's living room. I remember seeing my first surf movie with Jimmy at the Buckheart House. It was so cool, seeing the surf movies and hanging out with the older guys. I can't remember which movie it was that we saw the first skateboards they called bunboards. What a cool thing! It was a little like surfing. Made from about sixteen inches of two-by-four, add an old skate to the bottom and you were in business. I think that the first time I tried one, I was hanging with Jimmy at Pleasure Point when Rich Novak drove up in his white Ford convertible with a surfboard sticking out of the back seat, and showed us a skateboard like we saw in the movie. He let us try it on the sidewalk in front of the store. We were stoked! Needless to say, we soon made our own."

After seeing the bun boards in the movie with Davey, I remembered the old skate crate I had built years earlier. It finally clicked: you don't need the crate; you ride it like a surfboard! We got some old roller skates and nailed the front and back section to some two-by-fours, bending the nails over to hold them. We were stoked! We would skate the sidewalks along Pleasure Point Drive and on the cement area in front of the Pleasure Point Market. Those were some of the only sidewalks around on our funky side of town. We practiced maneuvers like we saw in the movie, and soon more bunboarders appeared.

The sidewalks at Pleasure Point, unfortunately, were flat; it was mostly about hills in those days. We frequently found ourselves across town on Beach Hill, which became the most popular skateboarding site in town. There were more bunboards than ever there, and having O'Neill's Surf Shop shack and Cowell's Beach right there fueled the fire. It was a short walk from Santa Cruz High

"...we, as pioneers, pushed the envelope, always looking for steeper, longer, and faster hills."
-Big John Evenson

School, so we bunboarded there after school almost every day. Our friends would all be there. Beach Hill was actually a formidable challenge, not so much for the steepness, but for negotiating the sharp corner and parking meters at the bottom. The old metal wheels, narrow trucks, loose ball bearings, and loose nails made a sketchy trial out of keeping control, and many bunboarders found out fast where the name came from.

A new shopping center construction started near my house. Once the parking lot was paved with smooth asphalt surfaces it opened a world of activity for my friends and me.

DAVEY SULTZER: "Jimmy and I found some good places to skate, or go bunboarding, as we called it. Fairly close to his house we found some really smooth cement to the drive-up window between the Wells Fargo Bank and El Rancho market. It was covered so it was cool and shady which was great on hot days, and we pretended it was a big tube. We hung out in that parking lot quite a bit when there wasn't any surf, and just go across a little creek to get something to eat at his folks' house. We also made a ramp at my house. We found a thick sheet of plywood that my dad had laying around a sawhorse, and we were good to go. We would just come down the ramp at a reasonable clip and skate down the street. No one thought of going up the ramp yet, that was many years down the road. The fact that we could actually turn them, a little like a surfboard, was ultra-cool. We were bunboarding at the El Rancho shopping center after school one day, at the bank now where Coffeetopia is located. It was the cool place because there was a banked corner there. I was going around the corner doing a head-dip, when all of the sudden I ran head first into a post. It was a serious wipeout. I remember Jimmy came running over thinking that I, at the least, had cracked my head open. He was saying, "Davey, Davey, are you OK?" There I was lying on the cement in serious pain, but it wasn't my head. That didn't even faze me. The problem was that I landed on my left wrist and broke it. It took a month or so to heal and that was the end of the bunboard thing for me. I decided to stick to surfing, which was a lot safer. We never became skateboard legends but Jimmy and I reached a level of proficiency in skating that has kept us going through life."

BIG JOHN EVENSON: "After the woody, a friend of mine had a '50 Ford, two-door business coupe for sale. It was lowered as low as it would go after cutting off the rubber stoppers. This was a highly technical job, heating the spring 'til it stopped going down. It had a dark purple body with lavender scallops. It had Buick portholes mounted in the hood that lit up; the front grill was changed to a '51 and it was named "Ambrose the Purple Mouse", lettered on the front fender behind the wheel well, polished off by 3/4 length side pipes and polished disc hub caps. Jimmy at the time was using his mother's liquid embroidery pens and applying his artwork on t-shirts. He had done a nice piece of "Ambrose" on the t-shirt. One day while pushing the envelope, my friend, David Stearns took us to the top of Vine Hill Road and followed me riding my bunboard at least 2 miles down hill at speed. David said his speedo registered 35 mph. Then the asphalt had pushed up into a washboard surface, which caused me to fishtail and unload. After 2 giant steps, I went end over end, breaking my wrist and ending my skateboard career. Worse than that, I shredded that beautiful t-shirt. Later I got a cast up to my elbow, which was a clean white canvas for Jimmy. He painted a surfer cartoon on my forearm only he made him butt-naked, warts and all. As soon as my mother saw it she had a fit and made me go back and have Jimmy paint on a nice pair of hibiscus baggies over the offending area."

ROAD RIDER WHEELS

1960s to '70s

During the 1960s, my bunboarding friends were dropping out like flies. It seemed like everybody but me had broken wrists. Surfing has its dangers, but falling off usually meant swimming and not eating gravel. Subsequently, my friends and I surfed most of the time and we went on numerous surf trips. One such trip was to Southern California, which was Mecca to surfing in California. While surfing the beach breaks there we met some members of the Playa Del Rey Surf Club who let us stay at their parent's homes. Later, while hanging out in the parking lot, we were impressed by their advanced skills with what they called "skateboards". Also of interest to us was their up-to-date equipment, which in those days meant clay wheels. Of course we had seen plenty of clay wheels, made-for-skateboard trucks and laminated, shaped decks, most of them pictured in the early surfing magazine ads. These advanced products were not common in Santa Cruz yet. Before long, the club visited our homes and our home breaks. Eventually two of the club members, Norman Walker and Frank Findlay, rented a house at Pleasure Point. We became close friends and they inspired my skateboarding. Norman amazed me with his arching soulful grace. He would ride barefoot on flat sidewalks, seemingly never having to push, just leaning, turning and twisting for momentum. He could borrow some cruddy plank and make it seem smooth. I tried one of them afterwards and it seemed too funky to ride. This era was epochal. It was a period of relative skateboarding perfection, after persevering years of sidewalk surfing. Daring challengers overcame the perils of dangerous equipment and terrain, unsung pioneers. But everything was about to change.

In 1965 skateboarding seemed to die out., except for Jan and Dean's "Sidewalk Surfing" playing steadily on the radio, I was awarded a scholarship to attend California College of Arts and Crafts, which meant moving from the beach to city life, where skateboards, at the time, didn't exist. After art school, I pursued an art career and by the early seventies had established a free-lance art service. In 1975, one call for service was from two guys I knew from my early surfing days, Rich Novak and

Jay Shuirman. I had previously designed the sticker logos for their small Solar Surfboards company, and years earlier had worked for Novak who was a partner at Olson Surfboards. Now they were developing a skateboard wheel out of the new urethane. A chemist named Frank Maceworthy had recently developed the formula and went on to establish Cadillac Wheels, the first urethane skateboard wheel. But the Cadillac wheels had loose open ball bearings like the old days, and were easily fouled by dirt. Novak and Shuirman formed NHS, and developed the first sealed precision bearing skateboard wheel, which was called Road Rider.

My first assignment for NHS was a logo and t-shirt for Road Rider. For the logo, I did classic style, hand-lettered Ritz-style slanted lettering with wings coming forward from the tips of the R's. For the T-shirt, I drew a girl skating slalom style down hill under the logo This relatively tame design was in deference to the laid-back surfer style of the day, because it was a period when skateboarding was dominated by surfers. Skateboarding would have to wait until the next generation to cross the land. Unadulterated by surfing culture, they would grasp the concept afresh and carry a new torch.

Demand for my time at NHS grew to the point where I asked for a base amount of work to schedule into my other freelance work. Skateboarding did not appear to be an open door for graphic art.; it was just a commercial job for me. I had been doing rock posters on the side, which allowed for almost unlimited freedom of artistic expression. But rock poster pay was low and the skateboard work steady, and I had a young family so I began to dedicate myself to it. Most of my early skateboard designs were logos, and the application was usually advertising in some of the first skateboard magazines that were starting up. But even within a logo, I always tried to find ways to be creative and then do my best. And after all, these logos were beginning to be seen around the world.

DAVEY SULTZER: "Jimmy's talent was more than established even at an early age. I'm fortunate to have been able to watch his abilities grow right up to adulthood. My favorites are his skateboard designs. I think his most impressive skateboard design is the logo he designed for Santa Cruz Skateboards. I can't say why it is, but

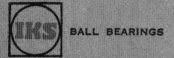

it grabs your attention from fifty yards away in a crowd. I can add that I've had this happen from Buenos Aires, Argentina; to Warsaw, Poland, and too many points in between to mention. It's really strange how that works, certainly it's on another level of commercial art."

Road Rider Wheels swept the industry, and they followed the Road Rider 2 wheels with Road Rider 4s, and branching out everywhere. Soon enough, they decided to make decks and named the new division Santa Cruz Skateboards. I was swept up enough about it that I got some of the early decks, which were made of pultruded fiberglass. I brought home a 27-inch board for me and a 19-inch model for my son, Jimmy. He was around eight years old then, and not yet known as Jimbo. Both decks had Road Rider 2s on them and the narrow trucks of the time. I knew right away they needed kick-tails. I brought it up at work, but no one I talked to seemed to care. I took the matter into my own hands and drilled a hole in the tail of my board and screwed a big nut and bolt through it, to act as a stop for my back foot. I glued a little rubber stopper on Jimmy's. They worked great. I put two strips of grip tape on each one and painted a little lightning bolt on the nose of his. Everything surfing seemed to have lightning then. Jimmy and I went out skating wherever we could find big parking lots. Big parking lots meant there were usually spacious unused corners without traffic and very smooth pavement. There were no prohibitions or "No Skateboarding" signs, and no one seemed to really care or even notice. We went out the first few times on the Sears corner lot on 41st Avenue, right down the street from our favorite surfing breaks.

JIMBO PHILLIPS: "I still have my first skateboard. I got it when I was about eight years old. My dad started working for NHS - Santa Cruz Skateboards. One day he brought home two brand new complete setups, one for me and one for him; his was yellow, mine was red. They were small fiber-flexy surf-shaped Santa Cruz boards with Road Rider 2 wheels. They didn't have kicktails so we glued rubber stoppers on the tail so your foot wouldn't slip off. There were no graphics except for Santa Cruz Skateboards written out in plain text."

There wasn't a surge of local skaters at first. After all, how many worked at the only skateboard company in town, like I did? Nobody did, except the secretary and Tim Piumarta. I had some of the first Santa Cruz boards of the urethane revolution, but there were hardly any other skaters around or many skating spots being used. But that worked fine for me because I was able to skate and spend quality time with my family.

Some of the first magazine ads for Santa Cruz Skateboards, 1976-77.

Photos by Dan Devine

TEAM SANTA CRUZ
Scott Sommers 1ST, Tony Carter 2ND, Mike Ashworth 3rd (L to R) junior men's slalom, World Pro-Am Hang Ten Skateboard Championships, John Hudson, Coach

Santa Cruz Skateboards

Santa Cruz Skateboards, The finest in pultruded fibreglass flex boards use Road Rider No. 2 wheels and Suregrip trucks. 24 inch . . . 39.95. 27 inch . . . 40.95. Road Rider No. 4 wheels w/rubber spacers add 5.00. Add 4.00 for Bennett trucks. Include 2.00 for shipping. Calif. add 6% tax.

SANTA CRUZ SKATEBOARDS,
745 41st Ave., Santa Cruz, Ca. 95062

SANTA CRUZ SKATEBOARDS

SANTA CRUZ SKATEBOARDS OFFERS A FULL LINE OF SUPERLIGHT, DURABLE EPOXY/GLASS WITH HARDWOOD CORE FLEX BOARDS.

SANTA CRUZ SKATEBOARDS INTRODUCES THE NEW HARDWOOD KICKTAIL SKATE-BOARD TOP WITH RABBETED UNDERSIDE FOR FULL MANEUVERABILITY.

PUT YOUR OWN SKATEBOARD TOGETHER BY ORDERING FROM THIS LIST, ASSEMBLY FREE.

SKATEBOARD TOPS
EPOXY/GLASS W/HARDWOOD CORE
(Kicktail and John Hutson Cutaway models shown at left in photo.)
Standard 24"-26½"
Cutaway 26½"-28½" $25.00
Kicktail 26½"-28½" $25.00
Screws included.

HARDWOOD KICKTAIL
(shown in photo right)
27"-$16.95, 29"-$17.95, 32"-$18.95
Nonskid taped 2.00 extra. Screws included.

WHEELS (IKS Bearings included)
Road Rider No. 2
Road Rider No. 4 . . . . 4.50 ea.
Road Rider No. 6 . . . . 6.50 ea.
New Road Rider Henry Hester Wheel . . 7.50 ea.
1½" wide, 2 7/16" tall
OJ Superjuice . . . . 6.50 ea.
OJ Slalom . . . . 6.50 ea.

TRUCKS (2 per board needed)
Tracker
Tracker Half Track . . . . 10.95 ea.
Bennett Hijacker . . . . 9.95 ea.
Bennett Pro . . . . 7.95 ea.
HPG Gullwing . . . . 9.95 ea.
Calif. Slalom . . . . 15.95 ea.
Road Rider Riser Pads (½") . . . . 7.50 ea.
Rad Pads . . . . 2.00 pr.
. . . . 4.50 pr.

ACCESSORIES (All items post paid in U.S.)
Santa Cruz T-Shirt (3-color design)
(Specify s, m, l) $6.00
Santa Cruz T-Shirts (3-color design)
(Specify s, m, l) $6.00
Henry Hester Poster . . . . . . 1.95 ea.
Road Rider Poster . . . . . . 1.95 ea.
Road Rider Decals . . . . . . 1.95 ea.
Anybody's Skateboard Book by
Tom Cuthbertson 50
Robinak Skate Pack 1.50
Road Rider Skateboard Pendant . . 16.95
. . . . 2.95

SAFETY EQUIPMENT (A Must)
Helmet (Norcon Made of Polycarbonite) . . $9.95
(Specify s, m, l)
Elbow or Knee Pads . . . . . . $5.95 pair
(Specify extra sm, s, m, l)
First Aid Kit $3.50

SHIPPING —Please include for postage and handling:
Skateboards — 2.00, Foreign — 5.00
Wheels/Trucks/Helmets - 1.50, Foreign — 3.00
Accessories/T-Shirts — Post paid in U.S., Foreign — 1.00
Enclose check or for fast delivery send money order
(Foreign payable with international money order)
No cash please, plus postage and handling.
(Calif. residents add 6% sales tax).

FREE! with skateboard order —
Anybody's Skateboard Book by TOM CUTHBERTSON!

SANTA CRUZ SKATEBOARDS
825 41ST AVE., SANTA CRUZ, CA.
95062 (408) 475-9434

IKS   OJ WHEELS   TRACKER TRUCKS   ACS   ROAD RIDER

PHOTO/METIVER

Disposable

Pre screen-printing deck, 1976.

JIMBO PHILLIPS: "We started out skating on the sidewalk across the street from our house. We were sort of the neighborhood pioneers, lucky to have a sidewalk with a slight hill and nice curbs. The house right across the street had the best driveway. It was wide and open flat cement. You could shoot down the hill on the sidewalk and ride into the driveway and do a big slash. We would also do catamaran runs were you both sit on your boards, cross legs, hold hands and lean to turn the boards together down the hill. It was lots of fun and we would have the funniest wipe-outs. Soon we moved on to local schoolyards. We were in close proximity to two schools. Live Oak school had super smooth hallways to shoot and a banked curb where the busses unloaded. I remember one day skating with my dad. We were bombing this hill at Harbor High school. I was at the bottom of the hill watching him come down, bombing fast, when he hit a rock and went into a Pete Rose slide on the rough gravelly concrete. He got a huge palmy salami on his hand and a chin chunk out of his Grizzly Adams beard. I remember he was worried about messing up his drawing hand. I can't blame him. I think the same thing

SANTA CRUZ SKATEBOARDS

1976

Top: First Santa Cruz stickers, eventually to be screened onto decks, 1976.

Center: Rebound Trucks stickers, 1976.

Jim Phillips' personal skateboards from the era,
Right: Yellow 26" pultruded fiberglass, 1976,
with Road Rider 2 wheels.
Left: 26" epoxy laminate, 1978.

1978

some-
times now. I
have broken my arm
skating before and I don't
want to mess up my drawing
hand because if I injure my hand, I'm
out of work."

Jimbo seemed to have a natural balance and
took to skateboarding fast. We ripped on virgin
parking lots. I made some little cardboard cones and set
up slalom courses. We had the best father and son time you
can have. Dolly caught on and decided it was an opportunity to go
shopping at malls that were springing up everywhere. It made for a solid
family trip, she could shop and we'd skate all over the parking lots, ramps,
and sidewalks. We tried to be respectful of shoppers, but it is entirely possible
that we had something to do with the "No Skateboarding" signs appearing in

17

SANTA CRUZ SKATEBOARDS

LAMINATED UNDER HEAT and PRESSURE!

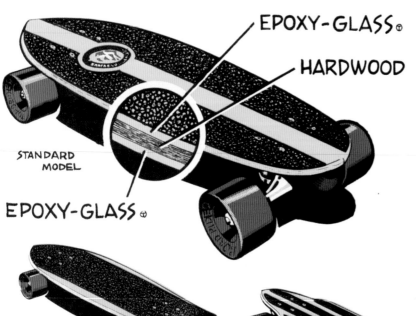

EPOXY-GLASS ®

HARDWOOD

STANDARD MODEL

EPOXY-GLASS ®

KICKTAIL MODEL

CUTAWAY MODEL

IKS BALL BEARINGS

©1976 NHS INC.

CAMBER

SANTA CRUZ SKATEBOARD TOPS ARE LIGHT-WEIGHT, LESS THAN HALF THE WEIGHT OF PULTRUDED BOARDS. HARDWOOD AND UNI/BI·DIRECTIONAL EPOXY-GLASS ® ARE LAMINATED UNDER HEAT AND PRESSURE FOR MAXIMUM STRENGTH AND FLEX RETURN. AVAILABLE IN: STANDARD ʷ/CAMBER, CUTAWAY ʷ/CAMBER, AND KICKTAIL, FLAT ʷ/KICK. STANDARD HIGH QUALITY MODEL AVAILABLE WITH HIGHEST PERFORMANCE TRUCKS AND WHEELS. SEE YOUR SKATEBOARD DEALER FOR MORE INFO! T-SHIRTS AND DECALS!

NHS INC
825 41ˢᵀ AVE
SANTA CRUZ, CA 95062
(408) 475-9434

TRACKER TRUCKS

oct, 76

18

One of the first Santa Cruz full page ads, October 1976.

later years. We had some favorite places around our area, some parking lots, a few drainage bowls, and the hill down into the lower parking lot of Harbor High School where we would go quite often. It was like a dream skating on wheels made from the new urethane. It can only be fully appreciated after using the earlier metal and clay wheels. The ride was solidly infectious, heart pumping, and sweaty. I skated like I could never have imagined back in my bun-boarding days.

JIMBO PHILLIPS: "We would take family trips to the big malls over the hill where my mom would go shopping and my dad and I would skate the surrounding parking lots. There weren't any "No Skate-boarding" signs or even security guards to stop us. It was great! We would find smooth sidewalks and banks behind the loading docks and session for hours. We used to frequent Frederick Street Park near our house quite often. It had a fun little cement bowl to skate down by the harbor. Many times my friends and I would hop in the back of my dad's truck, "Rosie" with our gear and he would take us there for a day of fun. I would love skating to the bottom then turn around and watch my dad come down. He would come carving down the line with a smooth surfy style, banking off the top of the bank then pumping back down for the speed run. He taught me how to do "Berts" and other carving maneuvers at that park. It was made of real ruff concrete, so the Road Riders worked great there. It's still there to this day."

Jimbo

Eight year old Jimbo Phillips, and his first skateboard, 1976.

My re-entry into skateboarding, like most others re-energized during the urethane revolution, was based mostly on surf-riding techniques; carving, cut-backs and nose riding. Because the wheels were so smooth riding, I was drawn to what I called in surfing, "climb and drop". That is a series of surfing maneu

PRO-FLEX
SANTA by CRUZ
SKATEBOARDS

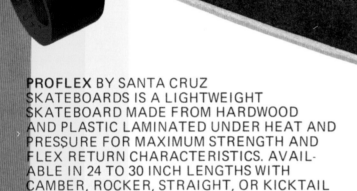

PROFLEX BY SANTA CRUZ
SKATEBOARDS IS A LIGHTWEIGHT
SKATEBOARD MADE FROM HARDWOOD
AND PLASTIC LAMINATED UNDER HEAT AND
PRESSURE FOR MAXIMUM STRENGTH AND
FLEX RETURN CHARACTERISTICS. AVAIL-
ABLE IN 24 TO 30 INCH LENGTHS WITH
CAMBER, ROCKER, STRAIGHT, OR KICKTAIL
MODELS.

AVAILABLE WITH ROAD RIDER WHEELS AND TRACK-
ER TRUCKS . . . THE CHOICE OF PROFESSIONALS.

SANTA CRUZ SKATEBOARDS

A DIVISION OF NHS INC.

825 41st AVE., SANTA CRUZ, CA 95062 • (408) 475-9434

A Phillips illustration would frequently be required when a product wasn't ready for the ad deadline.

Rhyn Noll

vers along a long walled-up wave. You drop, using gravity, to gain enough speed to propel the surfboard off the banked bottom and up across the face, and then repeat. It's a simpler form of the bottom turn, which can generate powerful speeds. I repeated this method using gravity to pump and spring forward, sort of like slalom, and then I would like to pull a large roundhouse cutback at the end. The slight decline we were skating on parking lots made the pumping effortless, but there was always the danger of over-reaching the natural speed limit, and the narrow trucks on those skateboards didn't provide much recovery comfort. There aren't any photos of myself skateboarding from then. I was into the ride and really never thought about getting any photos. I like to feel that I was anonymously pushing some kind of envelope. There's a lot of hot pro skaters out there now, but I like to joke that since I started earlier than most of them did, there was some point in time where I was better than them.

I was a goofy-foot skater, also referred to as screw-foot, which are surfing terms for using your

Jim sets up lights for a magazine ad photo-shoot in the 41st Avenue NHS shipping room, circa 1977.

foot skateboarding added nothing to my regular-foot surfing, and even conflicted heavily. But, I believe that Dyslexia works as an advantage in art, if nothing else, by spinning you around just one more time.

The workload was growing at NHS and they had branched out in dozens of ways, including OJ Wheels, Rebound Trucks, Cell Block risers, and others to come, like Independent Trucks. Each one needed a logo, magazine ads, T-shirts and stickers and that kept me quite busy. I was doing an occasional rock poster and suggested doing some art on skateboards, but there was not a lot of precedent and thus it seemed unnecessary. The fiberglass boards gave way to wood decks, such as the Special (see page 32). The Special didn't have a kick tail, just a slight rocker like a surfboard, which seemed ineffective to me. Before long, the Maple 5-Ply came in, and it finally sported a proper kicktail; it was my next choice for personal use. I took home a blue 27 x 6 1/2 inch model (see page   ),and loaded it with Rebound trucks and OJ wheels. But there was hardly time to skate.

Throughout the 1970s, I was constantly angling to get some art on decks. Tim Piumarta asked for a graphic. I created a Dragon holding the Santa Cruz dot (see page 37). That was my earliest full-deck graphic. It was printed around 1979 on 8 x 30 inch wood blanks. I was so stoked to finally be able to do a full deck graphic, but I didn't realize then that it was obviously a management attempt at unloading obsolete wood blanks by dressing them up. Those blanks had no kicktail and sales for them were dead after the kicktail came out. You can't prop up a no-kick deck after everybody had kicktails just by throwing some art on it, even if it was a cool design. Apparently the concept of deck graphics was seen as a failure along with the failure in sales of no-kick decks. Full-deck art did not appear for a year or so, after wide boards became popular.

right foot forward. I was what the surfers call a regular-foot surfer. I started surfing goofy-foot but my friends told me to surf regular-foot because most of the breaks in town were "right-hand slide". A screw-footer has to look over his shoulder on "rights', which are waves breaking to your right as you surf. Goofy footers are usually left-handed people. With surfing, your talented foot, right or left, wants to do the steering. So then you surf with left foot forward if you are right handed. With skateboarding, it's generally the same except backwards, the talented foot still wants to steer but the steering foot is now in front so the other foot can be pushing from behind. Besides, for skateboarding it doesn't matter what side you mount your ride, it's the angle of the turf that screws you up. I started out a goofy-foot artist too, that is by drawing my first pieces left-handed. But my mom, herself being a lefty and challenged by things like scissors, moved my crayons into my right hand. A lifetime of confusing left and right has resulted in Dyslexia for me. My goofy-

Around this time, Jay Shuirman's pet project was the development of a new truck with independent suspension. He asked me to create a logo while he was working with local mechanical engineers on

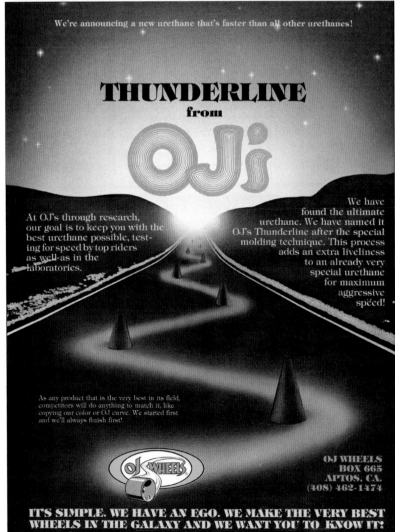

A few of the ads done during '77 and '78.

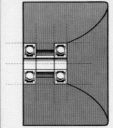

25

the stackable riser system

Matt French

THE SANTA CRUZ 5-PLY
This slightly flexible light-weight hat-
nate is available in two models: 27", 29".
WIDE BODY 5-PLY w/ROCKER, A
SLIGHT KICKTAIL. This board is excellent
carving and kick turn maneuvers in parks, poo...
and on banks. Rocker offers good foot hold and
stability with lower center of gravity.
WIDE BODY 5-PLY FLAT WITH KICKTAIL.
This all around board with more foot area and
wider tail is good in all terrain and excellent for
vertical. Flatness makes the board looser to kick-
turn while it will still carve to the limit.

JOHN HUTSON

THE VERSATILE JOHN HUTSON ENJOYS
THE "PERFECT TOUCH" OF HIS 5-PLY
IN PARKS, POOLS OR ON THE PAVEMENT.

SANTA CRUZ
DV 5
SKATE BOARDS

SANTA CRUZ ™

WHEELS (Bearings included)
...Road Rider No. 2, $5.00 ... No. 4, $7.00 ...
No. 6, $8.00 ... Road Rider Henry Hester,
7.00 ... Park Rider No. 4, $7.00 ... Logan 5,
.50 ... OJ's Superjuice, $7.50 ... Hot
ice, $7.00 ... Slalom, $6.50

TRUCKS (2 per board needed)
ound, $14.95 ... Tracker, $10.95 ...
cker Midtrack, $10.95 ... Tracker
track $9.95 ... ACS 500 Black & Silver,
5 ... ACS Black & Gold, $6.20 ... ACS
$8.50 ... Bennett Hijacker, $7.95 ...
nett Pro, $9.95 ... HPG Gullwing,
0 ... HPG Phoenix, $12.50 ... Calif.
, $7.50 ... Calif. Pro, $7.00 ... Calif.
Plate, $1.75 ... Rear
locks, $.50 ... Rad Pads, $4.50 ...

T-SHIRTS
$6.00 (Post paid in US) Santa Cruz Skateboa
Road Rider Wheels or OJ Wheels: Santa
Cruz Tennis Shirts, $9.95. Specify sizes xxs to xl

SHIPPING
Skateboards, $2.00, Foreign, $5.00 ...
Wheels/Trucks, $1.50, Foreign, $3.00 ...
Foreign T-Shirts, $1.00

Enclose name and mailing address, itemized order, check (or for fast delivery
send money order) including postage. Foreign payable with
international money order. No cash please. Calif. residents add 6% sales tax.

SANTA CRUZ

825 41st Ave, Santa Cruz, Ca. 95062 (408) 475-9434

prototypes. I liked working with Jay. I usually went in to the 41st Avenue NHS office at 9 o'clock every morning. Jay would pin my sketches and art on the wall and we would sit down together to look and talk about them. We would exchange ideas and he'd give me direction. It was that way with the Independent logo. I came in for several days with dozens of new sketches and they all went on the wall, but Jay kept sending me back to dig deeper. Among my sketches were some rising-suns and crosses, and I began toying with the iron, or Maltese cross which was long dead as the old '60s surfer's cross, and even longer dead as the biker's cross. I used a beam compass to make it into a round shape, which looked completely different than the old square iron crosses. During the sketch, I had a "Eureka" moment. I took my idea into the NHS office the next morning and it went on the wall as usual. Jay and Rich each stared at it for a while, and they both thought that it looked a little too "Nazi". My sketches were rejected and I was sent back to the drawing board. I went back to my studio determined to use it, knowing it was the one. I searched my archives and scrap file for some justification for using the symbol. I found a firefighter's logo, symbols on knights and Columbus' sails. Then in my scrap file, under the letter P, I found a Time Magazine cover of Pope John

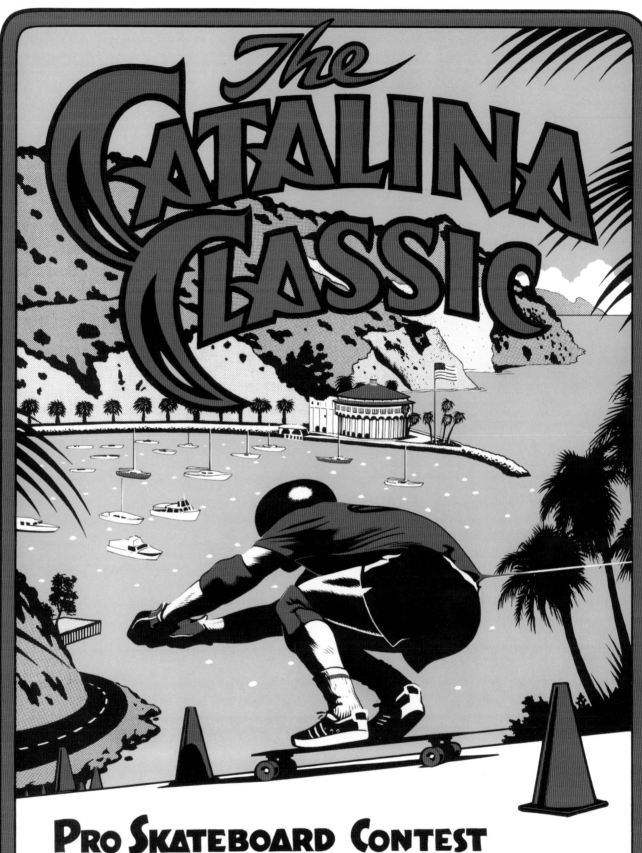

The Catalina Classic

PRO SKATEBOARD CONTEST

THRU THE STREETS OF AVALON, SANTA CATALINA

DOWNHILL
DUEL SLALOM
FREESTYLE EXHIBITION

OCTOBER **15·16** 1977 9 AM

INFORMATION: (714) 496·8611

© 1977 N+S GRAPHICS

Paul from the June 18,1979 edition. I was amazed; there was the cross on his vestments almost the way I designed mine. I marched into the office the next morning with the magazine to show what I thought was proof of acceptability. They both looked at each other and said, "Well, if the Pope has it, it must be okay!" That was that, and the Independent cross was born.

ED RIGGINS: "The Indy logo is one of the most hardcore logos in skateboarding, in fact it's almost as good as Thrasher." Ed Riggins is publisher of Thrasher Magazine.

"When I found the Time Magazine cover with the Pope wearing the cross just like the one I had drawn, I knew I had justification for it."
— Jim Phillips

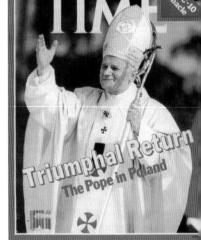

One of the first of many Indy ads done by Phillips.

THEY'RE #★X⚡!!! HOT!

Bobby Valdez. Powerflex Team. Hester/ISA Pro Bowl #3, Newark, Ca.

AVAILABLE IN 77MM AND 88MM.

"FLASH" 4 OUT OF THE TOP 8 FINALISTS AT THE HESTER ISA PRO BOWL#3 IN NEWARK, CA, RODE INDEPENDENT TRUCKS, INCLUDING WINNER BOBBY VALDEZ AND 2ND PLACE RICK BLACKHART.

Available thru **NHS**, Inc. 825 41st. Ave, Santa Cruz, Ca. 95062 408-475-9434

BUILT TO GRIND!™

"For this Indy ad, I was asked to use an expletive, but I talked them into using #*@!! instead. I found a good graphic symbol in my clip-file from a Time Magazine article entitled #*@!! Lawyers!"
- Jim

INDEPENDENT ™

TRUCK CO

✙ INDEPENDENT

TRUCK CO.

INDEPENDENT STAGE TRUCK COMPANY

INDEPENDENT ™

Some of the many hand-lettered logos created by Phillips for Independent.

BUILT TO GRIND INDEPENDENT TRUCKS

INDEPENDENT
SUPERWIDE
TRUCK COMPANY

INDEPENDENT

INDEPENDENT

RICH NOVAK: "By the end of the '70s we were rolling. We had Road Rider and we started the Independent brand. Jimmy was the creator for our icons, ads, and graphics. He pushed to put more art onto the skateboard, but we were reluctant to try. We'd use stripes and checkers, but nothing too radical."

I assumed, in my role as a graphic artist, that the deck art was my most important product, and I labored long into the night for many of them. Often, there was no way to handle the load unless I worked day and night. Since I was working out of my living room it was fairly convenient to keep going. Second to the decks, I considered the magazine advertising to be important, and spent a lot of time on the art and layouts, always looking for new ways to shred the borders. Today these techniques are everywhere, but there was a period when it was new and exciting. On one magazine ad, I taped the layout onto the bottom of a skateboard and had Jimbo grind around on it. For the ad, I drew a little guy grinding a curb with an arrow pointing to the border saying "Actually Grinded!"

the Dragon

The Dragon deck on the right is a composite made for this book, showing deck shape and graphic placement for an edition that is quite rare from 1979. This Dragon graphic image was taken from the board on the left to create this composite. The red board on right is a later re-use of the design, on a '80s "Stinger" model, probably a "one-off" using an old screen. The red board is the only existing sample of the Dragon graphic known to the author.

BILL'S WHEELS
Santa Cruz, Ca

Thanks to Brian Caldwell

Disposable

1979

JANTA CRUZ
SKATEBOARDS

JANTA CRUZ
U.S.A

**PRODUCTS
DISTRIBUTED BY
NHS DISTRIBUTORS**

ALVA ★ ACS
★ BEAR FOOT ★ DOG
TOWN ★ GULLWING ★ G&S ★
GYRO ★ HOBIE ★ HPG ★ INDE-
PENDENT ★ KANOA ★ KRYPTONICS
LAZER ★ LOGAN ★ MOLLY SHORTS
NORCON ★ ★ OJ'S ★ PARK RIDER ★
PROTEC ★ REBOUND ★ RECTOR ★ ROAD
RIDER ★ ROBINAK ★ SANTA CRUZ ★
SIMS (out of Calif.) ★ 3M ★ TRACKER

OLSON MODEL FOAMTAIL

SUPERJUICE ®

i-9434

OJ SLALOM ®   OJ SUPERJUICE ®

Introducing the **OJ SUPERJUICE** incorporating OJ's
phenomenal traction (they stick like tape!) with high speed
attained with a taller wheel. The OJ SUPERJUICE stands
2 5/8" tall with a 1 7/8" bite. The **OJ SLALOM** 2" x 2"
maintains its position as the best all-around O
complete line of wheels have the original O
performance proven design that allows whe
superior traction and speed over all other w
    OJ Wheels challenges any other manufact
develop a production wheel with as much tra
OJ's. "They stick like tape".
    OJ maintains exclusive quality craftsmanship
wheels are hand-poured into molds polished to m
like perfection. All wheels are unconditionally guar
for any defect due to workmanship. There has never
a defective OJ Wheel and there never will be.

OJ Wheels use IKS single sided sea
. The very best.
are recommend
Trucks

OJ W

Retail
OJ Wheels   **VAL Surf**
PO Box 665   PO Box 4003
Aptos, Ca. 95003   N. Hollywood, Ca. 9160

DEALER I

Dist., Richard Metiver, PO Box 665,
So. Cal. Tracker Trucks, PO Box 217, Caru

JANTA CRUZ
U.S.A

34

Tim Steenstra

SKATE SANTA CRUZ

STREET SKATE:

28½″ X 8½″, Flat Kick or Rocker Kick.

Three layers of maple veneer sandwiched and bonded with layers of Epoxy/Glass. Freestyle Rocker Model; (not shown) 27″ X 6½″, same construction as Street Skate. Designed for all types of Freestyle Skateboarding.

WIDE PLY:

28½″ X 9½″. 31″ X 10″

Our original ply laminate board with the bent tail. A great all around Park Board. Available with or without wheel wells.

STEVE OLSON MODELS:

30½″ X 9½″,
28½″ X 9¼″
Blocktail.

Designed and used by Steve to win the Hester Pro Bowl Championship. Available with or without wheel wells.

1979 GRAPHITE LOADED SLALOM BOARDS:

The lightest, fastest, most responsive slalom boards available.

John Hutson Cutback: Designed and used by John Hutson. This board has won more pro championships than any board made.

Henry Hester H-Bomb: Designed and used by Henry Hester to win the 1978 World Giant Slalom Championships.

The CAPITOLA CLASSIC

PROFESSIONAL DOWNHILL SKATEBOARDING

SEE THE THRILLS AND SPILLS OF HIGH SPEED PROFESSIONAL SKATEBOARDING
GUARANTEED PURSE $1750

REGISTRATION 7:45 RACING 9:30
MONTEREY AVENUE   CAPITOLA CALIFORNIA

AUGUST 30 1980

#1

BOB DENIKE
SECOND PLACE

JOHN HUTSON
FIRST PLACE

SEPTEMBER 3, 83

The CAPITOLA CLASSIC

& SANTA CRUZ - #

SANTA CRUZ

SKATEBOARD TOPS
EPOXY/GLASS W/HARDWOOD CORE...
$28.95 Standard 26" or 28", Cutaway 26½"
Kicktail 26½" or 28½". Screws & tape included
HARDWOOD WIDE 5-PLY LAMINATE
27"...$23.95...29"...$24.95...31"...$25.95.
Screws and tape included
GRAPHITE LOADED SLALOM BOARDS.
Hester H-Bomb, $55.00... Hutson Cutback.
$55.00... Hester Cruz Missile, $62.50.
Screws and tape included

DECALS
$.50 cents (post paid in US) Santa Cruz Skateboards,
Road Rider Wheels, Park Rider, OJ Wheels,
Tracker Trucks, Rebound or Cell Block

WHEELS (Bearings included)
Road Rider No. 2, $5.00... No. 4, $7.00... No. 6,
$8.00... Road Rider Henry Hester, $7.00... Park
Rider No.4, $7.00... Logan 5, $7.50... OJ's Superjuice, $7.50... Hot Juice, $9.00... Slalom, $6.50

TRUCKS (2 per board needed)
Rebound, $14.95... Tracker, $10.95... Tracker
Midtrack, $10.95... Tracker Halftrack $9.95
ACS 500 Black & Silver, $5.95... ACS Black &
Gold, $6.20... ACS 651, $8.50... Bennett Hijacker,
$7.95... Bennett Pro, $9.95... HPG Gullwing,
$13.50... HPG Phoenix, $12.50... Calif. Slalom,
$7.50... Calif. Pro, $7.00... Energy 5, $6.95...
Energy 6, $8.95... Energy 7, $7.95... Rear Skid
Plate, $1.75... Rad Pads, $4.50...Cell Blocks, $.50

Photo/Krizak

SAFETY EQUIPMENT Specify s, m, l
Norcon Helmet, $11.00... Premier Helmet,
$24.95... Norcon Elbow Pads, $13.95... Norcon
Knee Pads, $14.95... Mighty Mitt, $14.95 pr...
Rector Palm Pads Glove, $17.95 pr.

ACCESSORIES (Post paid in U.S.)
Anybody's Skateboard Book by T. Cuthbertson, $1.50
... Robinak Skate Pack, $16.95... Banner, OJ,Sierra
Cruz, Roadrider, Parkrider, $9.95.

T-SHIRTS
$6.00 (Post paid in US) Santa Cruz Skateboards,
Road Rider Wheels or OJ Wheels: Santa Cruz
Tennis Shirts, $9.95. Specify sizes and ad

SHIPPING
Skateboards, $2.00, Foreign, $5.00... Wheels/
Trucks, $1.50, Foreign, $3.00... Foreign T-Shirts,
$1.00
Enclose name and mailing address, itemized order, check (or
for fast delivery send money order) including postage and
handling. Foreign payable with international money order. No
cash please. Calif. residents add 6% sales tax.

825 41st Ave, Santa Cruz, Ca. 95062
(408) 475-9434

Send for product information and prices on
other products.

FACT? or FICTION?

Some manufacturers claim to make the fastest boards.
Some claim to make the racers choice.
Some claim to make boards that win.
Claims are claims... Facts are facts!

Let the facts speak for themselves.

In 1977 there were fourteen major pro races. Eleven of them were won on Santa Cruz boards!
The fact is, more racers are taking advantage of the boards that helped win those races, the same advantage that you get every time you step onto a Santa Cruz board!
Whether it be the rapid response from a graphite loaded slalom board or the perfect touch of the 5 PLY, take the advantage, take a Santa Cruz!

Steve Olson
Taking the Santa Cruz Advantage
at the Sierra Wave

Early in the 1980s,

...ushered in by the beat of new wave and punk rock music, wider skateboard decks and trucks appeared. The wide boards seemed to beg for adornment like a blank canvas, which an artist can't help but notice. I had wanted to fill that canvas for years. By this time, there were movements in art and music that were integrated into an emerging "pure" skateboarding culture, which led to a wider acceptance and demand for art. Steve Olson was a Santa Cruz team skater who began as somewhat of an NHS protégé; he was aboard while skateboards moved from slalom and parks to the street. He wanted full deck graphics, requested a checkerboard motif, and I was happy to be of service and finally able to get some art on a mainstream deck. There was a series of checkerboard Olson models, which I believe was a breakthrough by virtue of the amount of printed graphic art from nose to tail on them.

JIMBO PHILLIPS: "Skateboard styles quickly changed towards wider boards and trucks, along with bigger wheels and better graphics. My parents gave me a Steve Olson board for my twelfth birthday. It had Independent trucks and OJ wheels. I loved that board, it was big and tough with checkers on it and the Santa Cruz red dot logo. It had all the accessories on it: nose guard, rails, skid plate, grindmasters and a lapper. It was funny because I rode my board to school one day, and some of the other kids had Powell boards. I got into an argument with this one kid about which was better, Santa Cruz or Powell. It was definitely Santa Cruz!"

ROAD RIDER

Steve Olson
SANTA CRUZ
SPECIAL EDITION

Steve Olson

INDEPENDENT
TRUCK COMPANY

Free On The Streets

OK dad, so I put a Powell sticker over the Santa Cruz, what are you gonna do about it?

Jimbo & friend

Jimbo Phillips and Levi Gruys smirk at an authority figure, circa 1982.

Disposable

Tim Steenstra

40

STEVE OLSON SKATES

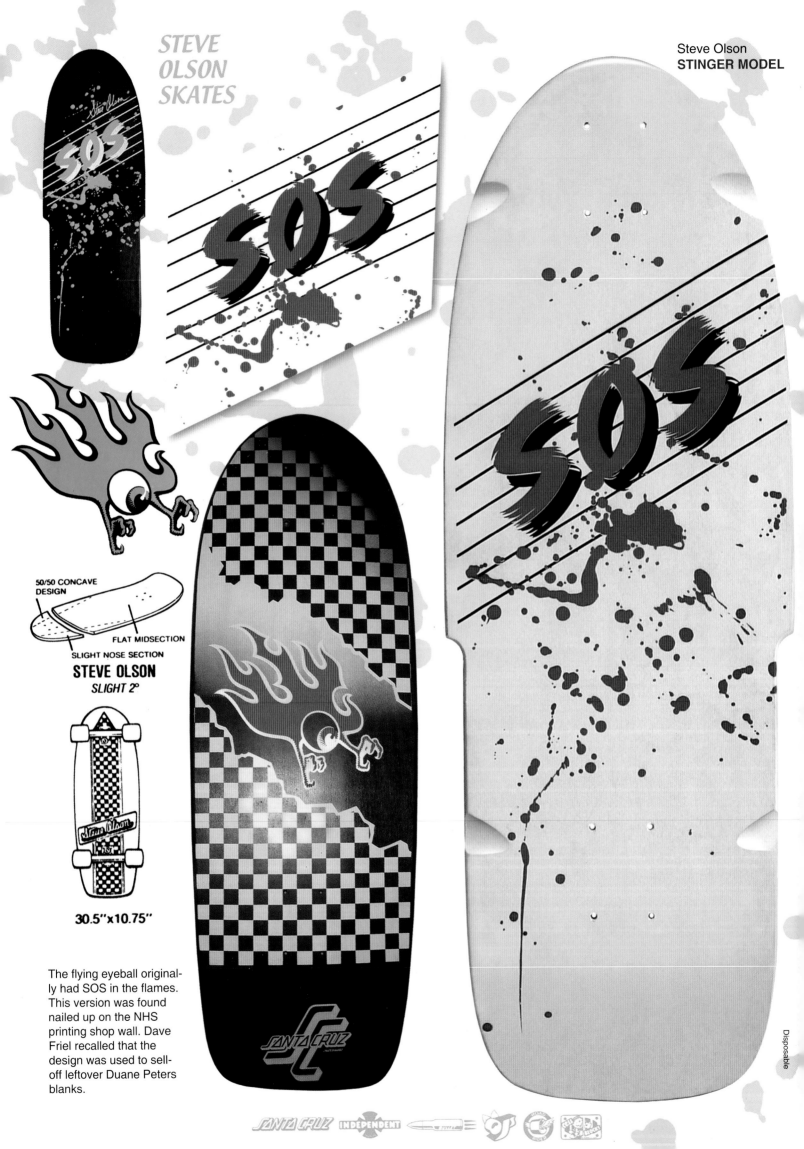

50/50 CONCAVE DESIGN

FLAT MIDSECTION

SLIGHT NOSE SECTION

STEVE OLSON
SLIGHT 2°

30.5"x10.75"

The flying eyeball originally had SOS in the flames. This version was found nailed up on the NHS printing shop wall. Dave Friel recalled that the design was used to sell-off leftover Duane Peters blanks.

SANTA CRUZ

Disposable

SANTA CRUZ INDEPENDENT OJ

Magazine ad of Duane Peters riding a Steve Olson.

Duane Peters soon came aboard at Santa Cruz and stretched the limits of that era when he asked for bold diagonal stripes. It was a period where the simplest statement would be seen as radical. There was not much graphic history so everything seemed new and different. These geometric shapes were a far cry from the graphics of today, requiring only a limited graphic ability, but it represented another brick in the wall for skateboard art. Along with other skateboard companies, the new wide-board graphics represented a breakthrough in bringing art to the streets and into the lives of some of the youngest and least powerful citizens. The early '80s was also a period where the tables turned, as skateboarding began to influence surfing in both performance and style. Surfers riding airbrushed surfboards with geometric new wave and punk day-glo colors were doing skateboard maneuvers, like aerials on waves, for the first time.

Steve Olson
BOMBER MODEL

Santa Cruz deck magazine ad, February 1980 .

NTA CRUZ STEVE OLSON MODEL
's own High Performance bank & pool design.
maple w/15" kick. (Shown w/169mm Indy Stage II
J. Double conicals)

SECOND GENERATION STREET SKATE
5/Ply maple laminate, full rocker w/kicktail—designed exclusively for today's street cruising (Suggested set-up: 131mm Indy's & O.J. Wheels)

E STINGER
back Design. light 7/Ply maple w/bottom finger wells—tapered for a strength. (Shown w/ 169mm Indy's & Blackhart wheels)

THE BEVEL by SANTA CRUZ
Functional New Parabolic design—concave deck w/upturned nose for ultimate footing! Ultra Stiff constr. Top/Bottom aerospace laminates over 5/Ply maple core. (Shown w/169mm Indy's Park Rider 4.5 Conicals)

SKATE SANTA CRUZ

THE BEST BOARD BUILT

MANUFACTURER & DISTRIBUTOR
MOLLY SHORTS

408 475-9434   824 41ST AVE SANTA CRUZ CA.   TELEX 171030

43

SANTA CRUZ

NEW FOR 1983!

ALL MAPLE LAMINATES!
EXCLUSIVE 3° UPTURNED NOSE
MEDIUM DEPTH 3° CONCAVE DECK

FLAT BASE AT KICK

15° KICK

TRI ANGULAR
CONCAVE DESIGN

MEDIUM
3°

NEW! D.P. CONCAVE

NHS Inc. 825 41st AVE, SANTA

SANTA CRUZ

DUANE PETERS

SANTA CRUZ
PRO SERIES

Disposable

Disposable

44

30.5"x10.75" & 29"x10.25"

BEVEL *MAXIMUM 6°*

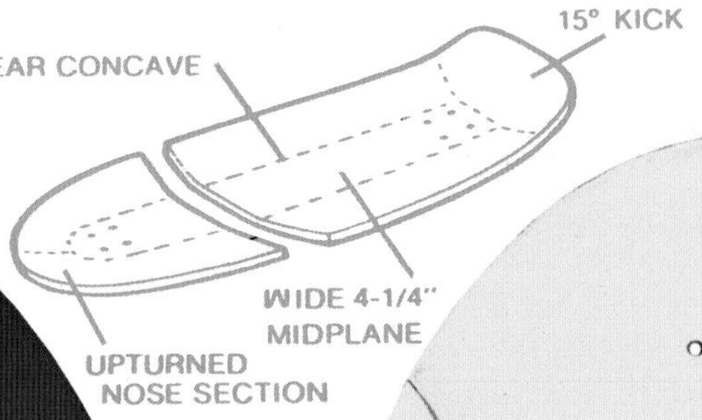

UNIQUE LINEAR CONCAVE

15° KICK

WIDE 4-1/4" MIDPLANE

UPTURNED NOSE SECTION

BEVEL SKATEBOARDS

SANTA CRUZ ™

SANTA CRUZ STINGER

Tim Steenstra

46

Disposable

SANTA CRUZ

SPECIAL
EDITION

SANTA CRUZ
7 PLY
CONCAVE

SANTA CRUZ STREET SKATE

CONCAVE

FREEDOM

SANTA CRUZ
STREET SKATE

SANTA CRUZ
NHS INC.
NHS, INC. 825 41st AVE, SANTA CRUZ,
CA. 95062 (408) 475-9434
SEND $1.00 for CATALOG, DECAL & ACTION PHOTO
ACTION NOW 53

Disposable

47

R/S 10" RAMPS/STREETS/BANKS 10"wide 30"long Ultra functional shape. $29.95

Tim Steenstra

R/S C 10"wide,30"long Linear Concave Design Medium 3° concave depth, 15°kicktail. Assembled $94.95 Deck only $34.95

Tim Steenstra

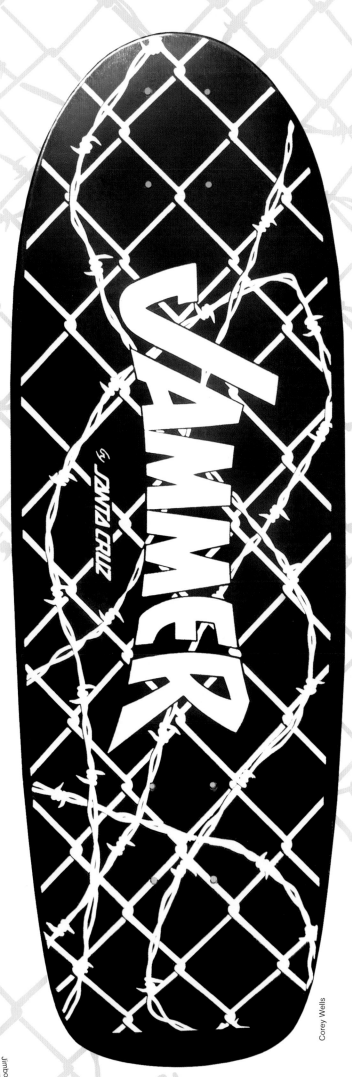

ne of the early
anta Cruz ads
Thrasher,
s one with
n's alma mater,
anta Cruz
gh School.

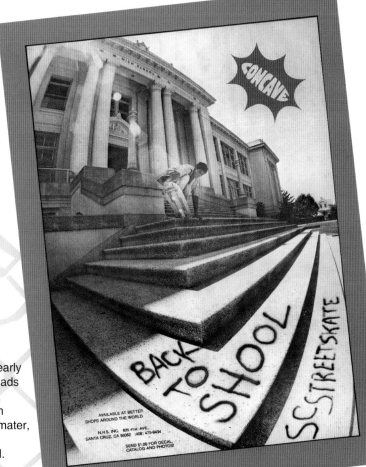

1981

Rob Roskopp DESIGNS by SANTA CRUZ

SANTA CRUZ

BIG ROSKOPP NEW SHAPE

SOQUEL DR. SOQUEL, CA 95073 (408) 475-9434

ROSKOPP STREET NOW AVAILABLE IN BLACKTOP (TM)

KEENAN

The Rob Roskopp deck graphic series was one of the outstanding sales leaders of all time at NHS. It started out without a clue of its future role in shaping the company's image. Rob was a good skater and sort of the next NHS protégé following Steve Olson. On his first team board, he asked for an arm sticking out of a target pointing to his name. NHS was starting to shake off a serious recession in the skate industry and at the same time dealing with the tragic loss of Jay Shuirman's untimely passing. The Roskopp board sold well enough that Rob was offered a new graphic the following year. NHS production manager, Tim Piumarta, called me into the office and simply asked me if I could do more, along the same idea. I made just enough of the creature coming out and it became a must-have for a generation of skaters. Over the next few years we repeated the idea process several more times with the III, IV, and V, and the rest is history. I was getting enthused, and the Roskopp designs enabled me some artistic freedom and a venue to create fairly wild stuff.

ROSKOPP Deck Decal 10.0" X 30.25"

Rob Roskopp DESIGNS by SANTA CRUZ

57

RICH NOVAK: "This is when Jimmy's art really started to click. He created the first graphics on skateboard wheels and he was finally given the chance to project the images he wanted onto skateboards. He did everything, and nothing was off-limits. His art was the right art at the right time for the right market".

Screaming Hand came into existence around 1985. Speed Wheels Santa Cruz manager, Richard Metiver, had been building up the wheel division from nothing. His earlier line of NHS wheels, OJ became a victim of the late 70s recession. But he was back with OJ II, Bullet, Slimeball, and a few other lines, and his sales were up. He asked me to dream up a logo for his Speed Wheels line. I went home to my studio and I was sketching around. Your hands are always right there in front of you and it was something to draw. I made my hand clench to show angst, like I have drawn for years to represent someone drowning. My clenched left hand seemed to scream. With my right hand, I added a mouth and color penciled the flesh blue and the tongue red. I knew right then it was a killer logo and didn't bother with more ideas. The next morning, I took my sketch to the office where it was immediately approved. On the original hand sticker, the hand was coming out of a circle of spinning letters that read, "Speed Wheels Santa Cruz". On the next batch of stickers, Metiver asked for the letters to be on the palm like a road rash. It was enjoyable working with Rich; he has a great sense of humor and lots of ideas. We worked well together on some funny advertising for the wheels, as well as on his Rip Grip product line.

ROSKOPP TARGET
Santa Cruz Twin Kick
9 1/2 X 31 1/2"
5 1/8 & 6" nose

Santa Cruz Skate Shop

ROSKOPP by Santa Cruz

ROB ROSKOPP: "Jim Phillips was the most influential artist of the '80s. His deck art set Santa Cruz Skateboards apart from every other skate company and was a huge factor in their overall success."

As it turns out, my pen and ink graphic techniques turned out to be perfectly suited to skateboards because they were most often printed by silkscreen process. My style of thick and thin key-line drawing lent itself to a process that is highly inexact; especially when the item printed is not flat, such as convex deck bottoms. My childhood love affair with comic books and my subsequent emulation of their great masters waited without much purpose until skateboards came along. It was the perfect art technique to screen print and comics-style art was the perfect medium for communication and expression. When things go well, it's usually because of a chance meeting of diverse but compatible elements with cross-nurturing growth potential, and there were lots of those floating around those days.

Roskopp
street "mini,"
the natural is a first edition,
the yellow is a 30th Anniv. re-issue.

Disposable

Santa Cruz Skate Shop

vations as "written" orders. The only reason I could handle late ads along with large, high-detail graphics was because I worked late every night. But eventually, there were not enough wee hours to keep my job list short enough. The demand of forty or fifty million dollars in sales waiting for your next jewel can be taxing. I was trying to take care of every detail of advertising, making something in art that was effective according to the application, and satisfying myself with enough creative expression to stay motivated.

SEAN CLIVER: "Prior to winning my dream job as an artist in the skateboard industry, I worked at a skate shop in Madison, Wisconsin. During the wintertime, customers were few and far between, so many an idle afternoon was spent scrutinizing the graphics from various companies. Most decks were cut-and-dry screen jobs consisting of solid colors and simple black trap-lines, but I was consistently stymied by the colorful intricacies achieved by Jim Phillips with his creative mixture of line work and separations on the various Santa Cruz models. In the decades to follow, not one company ever came close to replicating the professional standards of Jim's work in what is fast becoming the lost art of deck screen-printing." Sean Cliver is author of Disposable: A History of Skateboard Art.

NHS was grossing forty million in yearly sales. The pressure was on. I had been keeping a list of the incoming job orders and worked on them one at a time. That's all you can do, right? Wrong. Jobs were continually bumped ahead in priority. And there was no way to reprioritize an ad. We were doing a dozen magazine ads every month, and each had a deadline that would cost thousands of dollars if missed. To make matters worse, almost every ad was dumped in my lap in the last days before the deadline. I always tried to carry the ball. I was dependable, so management underlings could fritter away the time and hand it off to me as a rush job. A rush job is nothing but stress. Eventually, I had to be like Mussolini making the trains run on time and I made the ads and photos get to me on time and instituted such amazing inno-

The Slasher was the Keith Meek pro model. Keith above and top right.

Corey Wells

THRASHER MAGAZINE: "Created in 1985 by illustrator Jim Phillips, the hand served as an overall brand image for the entire Speed Wheels line, which included Slimeballs, Bullets and OJs. With a blood-stained compound fracture, flapping tendons, and misplaced mouthpiece this aggro amputee became one of the most recognizable skate logos of all time."
May 2002, #256.

The original Screaming Hand logo, 1985.

The first Sreaming Hand stickers (left), were white vinyl. Subsequent stickers (right), were on clear mylar.

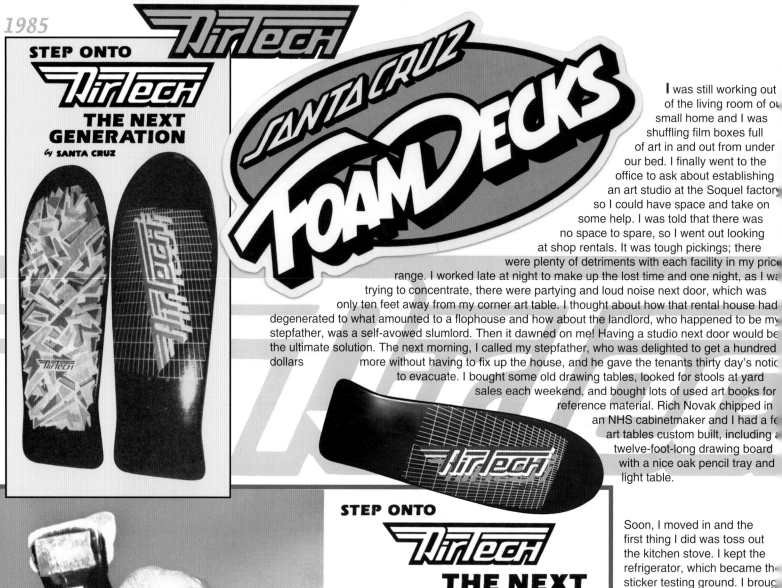

STEP ONTO AirTech

THE NEXT GENERATION

by SANTA CRUZ

SANTA CRUZ FOAM DECKS

STEP ONTO AirTech

THE NEXT GENERATION

by SANTA CRUZ

ROBBY BUTTNER, AMSTERDAM

I was still working out of the living room of our small home and I was shuffling film boxes full of art in and out from under our bed. I finally went to the office to ask about establishing an art studio at the Soquel factory so I could have space and take on some help. I was told that there was no space to spare, so I went out looking at shop rentals. It was tough pickings; there were plenty of detriments with each facility in my price range. I worked late at night to make up the lost time and one night, as I was trying to concentrate, there were partying and loud noise next door, which was only ten feet away from my corner art table. I thought about how that rental house had degenerated to what amounted to a flophouse and how about the landlord, who happened to be my stepfather, was a self-avowed slumlord. Then it dawned on me! Having a studio next door would be the ultimate solution. The next morning, I called my stepfather, who was delighted to get a hundred dollars more without having to fix up the house, and he gave the tenants thirty day's notice to evacuate. I bought some old drawing tables, looked for stools at yard sales each weekend, and bought lots of used art books for reference material. Rich Novak chipped in an NHS cabinetmaker and I had a few art tables custom built, including a twelve-foot-long drawing board with a nice oak pencil tray and light table.

Soon, I moved in and the first thing I did was toss out the kitchen stove. I kept the refrigerator, which became the sticker testing ground. I brought over a big bottle of peppers that I thought were too hot to eat, but eventually they became a staple among the studio artists. There were two small but prolific lemon trees in the front yard, so I kept a pitcher of lemonade in there, which was eventually replaced by the workers with Mountain Dew, when it became the studio drink. I painted the walls and made curvy shelves to save space. I made a small cement walkway over to my house because I was going back and forth so often tracking dirt into both. NHS paid the rent, but I called it Phillips Studios and began to look for young skateboarding artists. I had recently done a comic book called Road Rash, and used several young artists for skateboard stories. Naturally, I called on some of them. The first one I sought was my son Jimmy, but he had another job and was reluctant to leave it.

JIMBO PHILLIPS: "In my high school years, Santa Cruz were the boards to have. My dad was producing the sickest graphics in the skateboard market: the Roskopp series, Slasher, Salba, Grosso, and so on. Santa Cruz was on fire, so needless to say I was stoked when my dad got me my first job after my paper route at the factory sanding blank skateboard decks. It was cool being surrounded by skateboards, but sanding boards all day after school sucked big time. My first week on the job, I was sanding a board, when the strings on my sweatshirt got sucked into the sander and ripped my hoody right off my back and almost pulled me right into the machinery. The woodshop boss told me he's seen people lose limbs that way, so I guess I was lucky. Eventually I moved into the warehouse, assembling complete boards which was fun, but after a while working every day after school was cutting too much into my surf and skate schedule, so I quit."

OJ VERTICALS

SPEED WHEELS SANTA CRUZ

PHILLIPS

BULLET

FREAKS ON DISPLAY
TOP PRO SKATERS ABUSING THE NORM

SPEED FREAKS VIDEO

SPEED WHEELS SANTA CRUZ

board wheels
esy of Matt french
iends, including Matt weinstein,
Wells and Zack Garcia.

Disposable

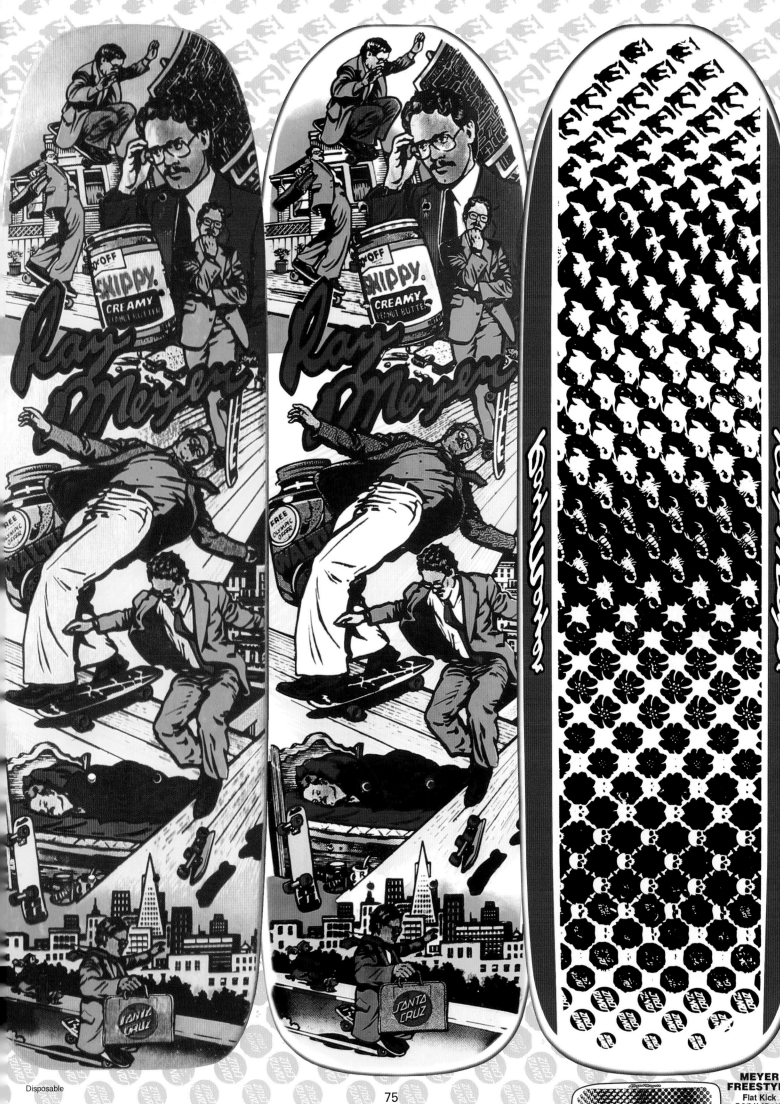

Disposable

75

MEYER FREESTYLE
Flat Kick
7 3/8 X 27 1/4"
4 7/8" nose

76

JEFF KENDALL

JEFF KENDALL

JEFF KENDALL

SANTA CRUZ
PRO SERIES

SANTA CRUZ

**KENDALL
SMALL**
Deck, T-shirt, Decal
9.5" X 29.75"
7/Ply & Blacktop

LIGHT'N UP

SANTA CRUZ

BOLD DESIGNS FOR SKATERS ONLY.

FILMHAUS-STUTTGART

CLAUS GRABKE

SC PROSERIES

Phillips Studios
1406 Webster St.
Santa Cruz, CA 95062

9 · 13 · 89

CLAUS

HERE'S A FEW SKETCHES I DID FOR
YOUR DECK. HOPE YOU LIKE EM.

ALSO ENCLOSING YOUR POSTER IN
CASE YOU HAVENT SEEN IT! HOPE
YOU LIKE MY TREATMENT OF COLOR
AND BORDER. NICE PHOTO

Danke

Jim

GERMAN
TEAM

CLAUS GRABKE ALLAROUNDMODEL

FRIEDRICHSTRA
70174 STUTTGAR

Tim Ng

GRABKE
STOCK
Control
X 31 5/8"
1/2" nose

GRABKE
LARGE
Deck, T-shirt, Decal
10.0" X 31.0"

**GRABKE
SMALL**
Deck, Decal
9.75" X 29.5"

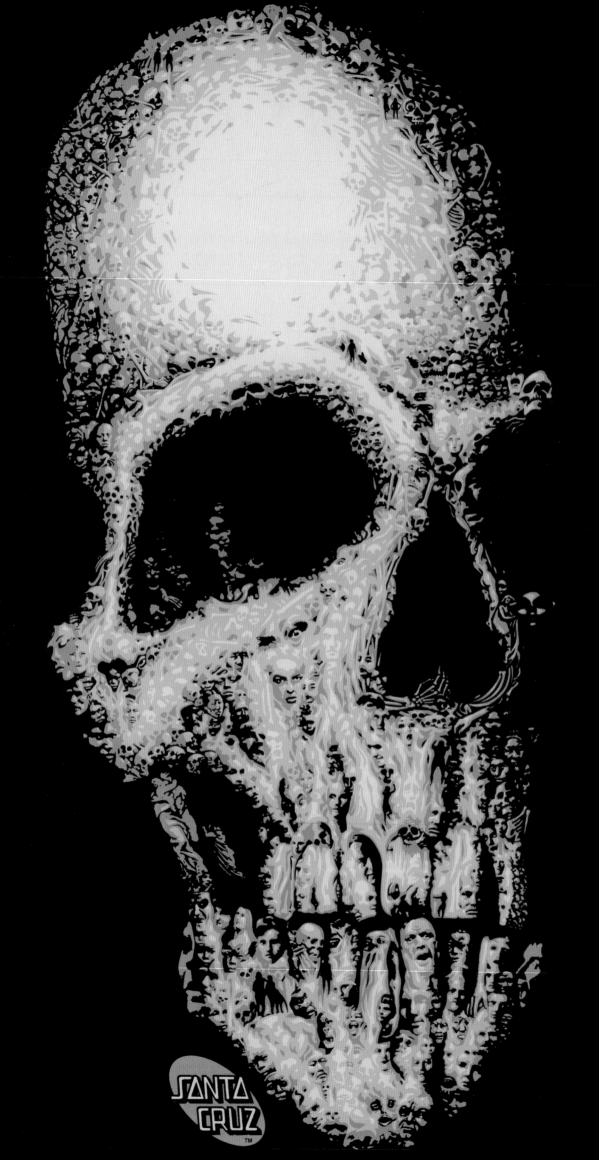

SANTA CRUZ

The
Skull

CREEP
T-shirt, Decal
.0" X 31.0"

SANTA CRUZ

GROSSO

JEFF GROSSO

SANTA CRUZ SKATEBOARDS

GROSSO MODEL SANTA CRUZ

JEFF GROSSO

MCMLXXXVI

GROSSO STREET
Deck
9.75" X 29.5"

88

holds the orignal art,
rubylith layers for the
sso Toybox deck, circa 1987.

JEFF GROSSO

JEFF SSO GROSS

ORIGINAL Formula

SC PRO SERIES

Disposable

Speed Wheels

Disposable

92

RANKINE
Deck
10.125" X 31.0"

Disposable

**JESSEE
SMALL**
Deck, Decal
10.0" X 30.0"

95

Jason Jessee

T-shirt, Decal
25" X 31.0"

SANTA CRUZ

PRO SERIES '86

99

S.ALBA

, T-shirt, Decal

.25" X 31.0"

Disposable

Disposable

101

Disposable

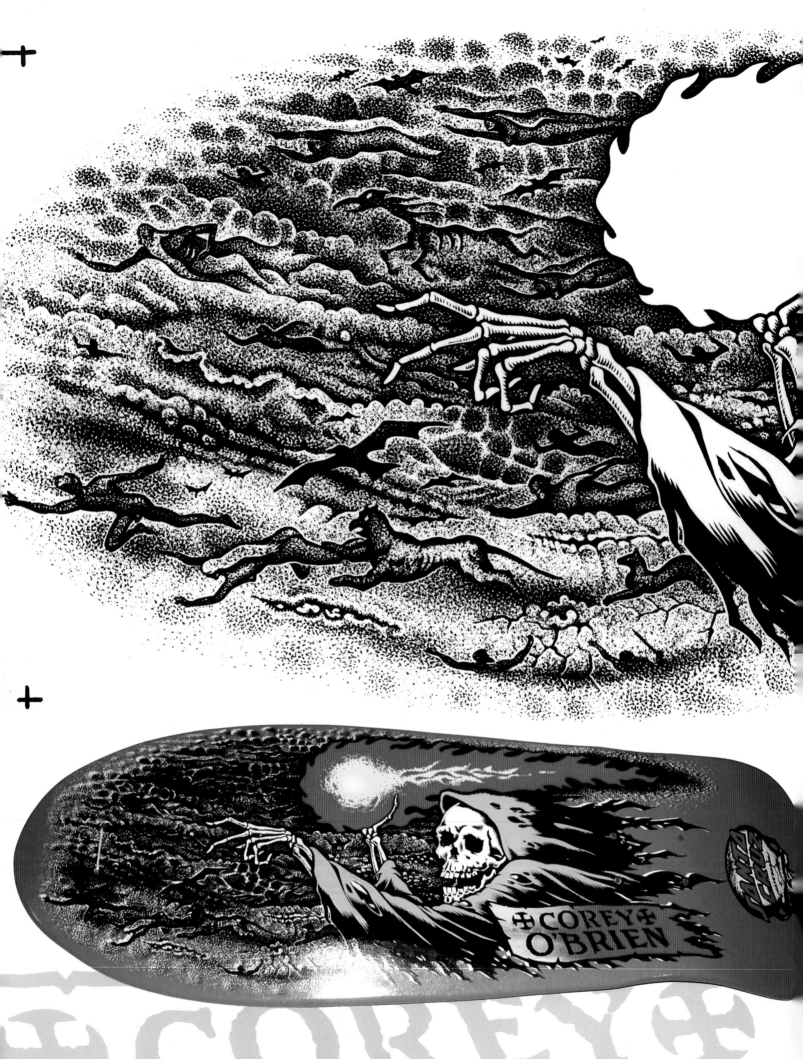

Mike McCarthy

BLACK

O'BRIEN
Deck, T-shirt, Decal
10.0" X 30.0

GRAPHITE SLALOM
Deck
8.0" X 28.0"

TOYODA
Deck
10.25" X 30.0"

PRO SERIES

AS SMALL
ck, Decal
" X 29.25"

HOSOI STREET MINI
Deck, T-shirt, Decal
9.5" X 29.75"

Disposable

112

HOSOI RAMP
Deck
5" X 31.0"

Disposable

HOSOI STREET
Deck, T-shirt, Decal
10.0" X 30.25"

the **Mонк**

Chris Chicarella

MINI
HAMMERHEAD
II

HOSOI

Disposable

Disposable

CHRISTIAN HOSOI

VERT MODEL

HAMMERHEAD

SKTBRDS

ROCKETS

SERGIE VENTURA HOSOI

HOSOI
SERGIE VENTURA
Deck, T-shirt, Decal
10.25" X 31.0"

Disposable

NEW MINI
GROSSO
by SANTA CRUZ
9¾ x 29½
"FOR ALL YOU..."

DECK
GROSSO
10.0" X 31.0"

PHILLIPS STUDIOS
JIMBO

ENJOY Jeff Grosso

SANTA CRUZ SKATEBOARDS

SANTA CRUZ

Jimbo

PHILLIPS STUDIOS
JIMBO

PHILLIPS STUDIOS
JUSTIN FORBES

Disposable

Disposable

GROSSO

ck, T-shirt, Decal

10.25 X 31.0"

GROSSO
SMALL

Deck, T-shirt, Decal

9.75" X 29.5"

121

PHILLIPS STUDIOS
JIMBO

ROSKOPP FACE II
Cruz Missile II
9 7/8 X 31 1/8"
4 1/2 & 5" nose

Disposable

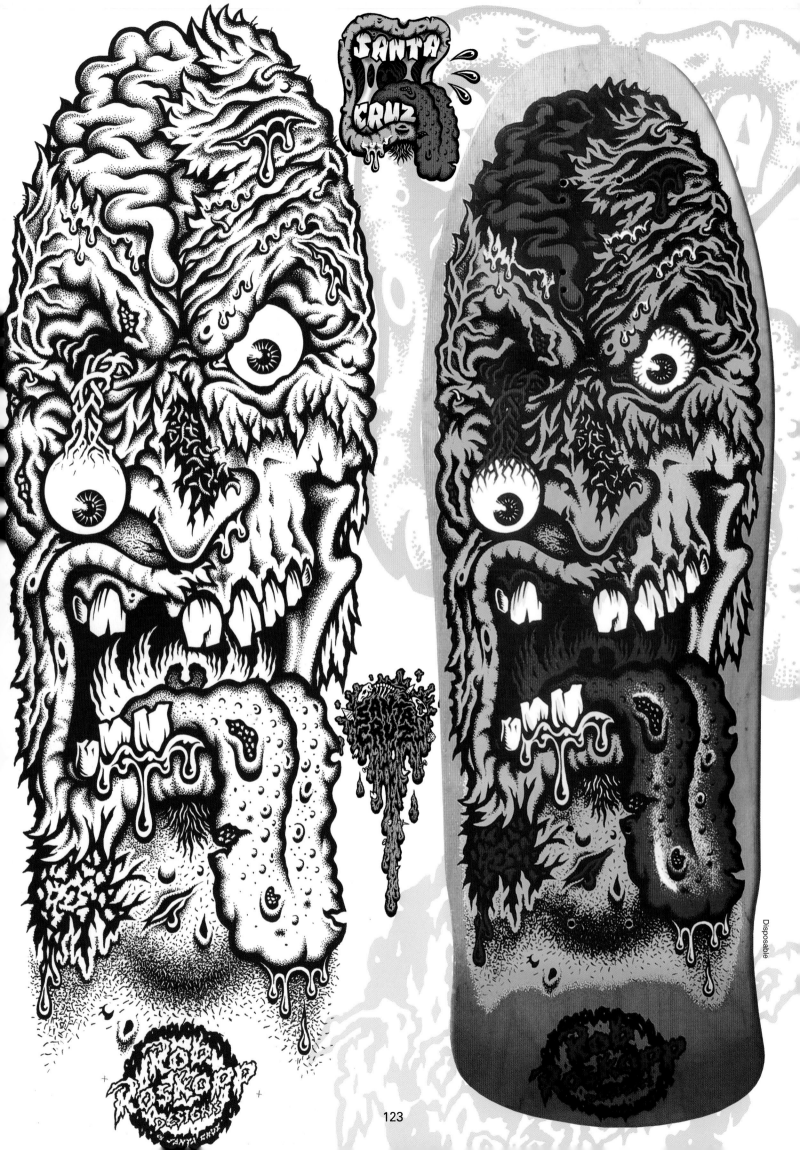

Disposable

SPEED WHEELS SCREEM

NATAS KAUPAS

SANTA MONICA AIRLINES

NATAS

NATAS

NATAS

Disposable

NATAS SMALL
Deck, T-shirt, Decal
10.25" X 30.0"
7/Ply & Blacktop

124

santa-cruz

SOREN AABY
SANTA CRUZ

SOREN AABY
1595
santa cruz

AABY SHIELD
ruz Missile II
10 X 31 5/8"
/4 & 5 1/4" nose

Santa Cruz

Disposable

JIM THIEBAUD
Deck, T-shirt, Decal
10.125" X 30.5"

HEDGES SYCHEDELIC
Cruz Missile II
10 X 31 1/2"
4 1/2 & 5" nose

SANTA CRUZ

John Munnerlyn works in Studio B on a Robert Williams inspired graphic to be made into a sticker.

Photo: Jim Byberg

Disposable

PHILLIPS
STUDIOS
MOJO

MIKE CONROY
SANTA MONICA AIRLINES

CONROY
WOMAN
Cruz Missile II
10 1/8 X 31 5/8"
4 3/4 & 5 1/4" nose

MIKE CONROY

SANTA MONICA AIRLINES

KENDALL LARGE
Deck, Decal
10.0" X 30.5"

SANTA CRUZ

CRUZMISSILE

Disposable

Disposable

129

**O'BRIEN II
SKELETONS**
Cruz Missile II
10 1/8 X 31 5/8"
5 & 5 3/4" nose

KNOX
GHOUL
Cruz Control
10 X 31 3/4"
3/8 & 5 7/8" nose

CRUZ CONTROL CONCAVE

CRUZ CONTROL CONCAVE

Disposable

Disposable

Photos by Jim Byberg

STUDIO *B* PHILLIPS STUDIOS Kevin Marburg

DRESSEN ROSES
Cruz Missile II
10 X 31 7/8"
5 1/4 & 5 3/4" nose

SANTA CRUZ

RIPGRIP
SANTA CRUZ

**NATAS
PANTHER**
Cruz Missile II
10 1/8 X 32 3/8"
5 3/8 & 5 7/8" nose

**BOYLE
STAINGLASS**
Cruz Missile II
10 1/8 X 31 3/4"
4 1/2 & 5" nose

Disposable

NATAS LARGE
Deck, T-shirt, Decal
10.25" X 30.0"

NATAS LARGE
Deck, T-shirt, Decal
10.25" X 30.75

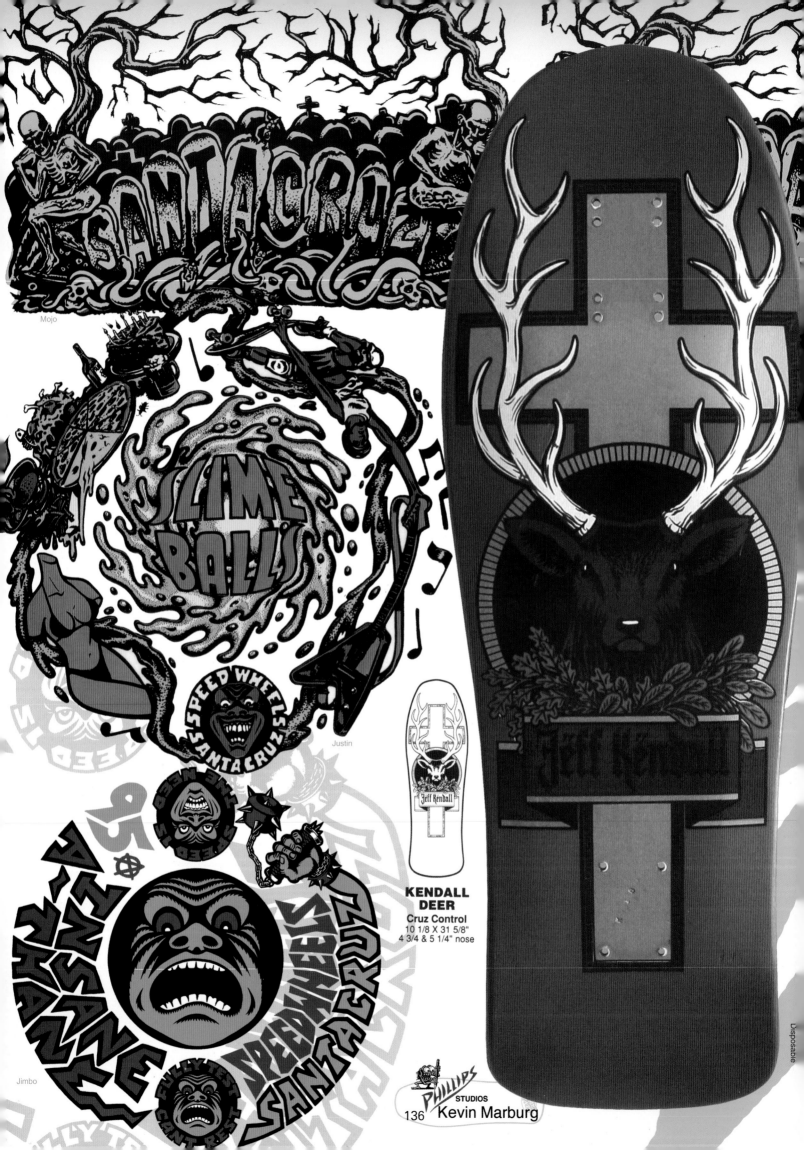

Mojo

SLIME BALLS

SPEED WHEELS SANTA CRUZ

Justin

Jimbo

Jeff Kendall

KENDALL DEER
Cruz Control
10 1/8 X 31 5/8"
4 3/4 & 5 1/4" nose

Disposable

The original Slasher design was ejected from the 3A committeee, aying it was not an image they anted to promote, so I knew it ould be perfect for skateboarders!"
Jim

Keith Meek

the "Meekster"

PHILLIPS STUDIOS
Keith Meek

CRUZ

SANTA CRUZ

Disposable

Seal of approval placed on decks in the late 80's.

Bush Hog truck bushings were from the Speed Wheels division 1989.

Malnufractured by Santa Cruz, a Christmas T shirt made by NHS in 1988, a collaboration of Jim and Justin.

Skate from liability sticker.

STUDIOS

Photo: John Munnerlyn

STUDIOS

Jimbo Phillips draws a wheel graphic on the light table at Phillips Studios, while job orders hang on the wall.

SKATEBOARDING IS NOT A CRIME

FORMATT

FORMATT

JIMBO PHILLIPS: "Right after graduating from high school, while taking art classes at Cabrillo college, the opportunity came up to do a comic strip for Road Rash Comix, which was a skate comic that Pops was doing with NHS. It payed a hundred bucks a page and was a really fun project with creative freedom, as long as it was about skateboarding. It was the first art job I ever got paid for and I was stoked."

The first studio artist that I hired was Justin Forbes. He had done an outstanding job on his road Rash assignment, and immediately impressed me with his drawing ability. He didn't need me to explain how to draw skateboard action. As a plus, Justin came with a sidekick, named Paul "Lousy" Hirscher. Lousy would just hang out and do whatever came up that was needed. I immediately put Justin on some drawing projects and soon we collaborated on a large piece for the Hosoi vert deck. He would draw on it during the day and I would draw on it at night after the studio was closed. We threw everything into that graphic, which started out as a rough sketch of Christian skating. We turned the elements into bananas, dice, and everything else we could think of. My son, Jimmy, saw the art fun we were having, so he quit his job and came to the studio to work for his dad. It was there he was dubbed with the nickname, Jimbo, which distinguished his name from mine.

quick and I got a lot better really fast. I'd been drawing my whole life and always had the talent, but creating finished graphics for production on products was a whole new level. I started off doing small lettering and characters for the corners of catalogs. Some stuff would never even get used, and sometimes you'd have to redraw it ten times, but It was great practice anyway."

One of Jimbo's friends, Andreas Ginghofer, was sort of artistic. His dad, Ray Ginghofer, painted murals and did pencil portraits at one of the nicest restaurants in town. Although Andre didn't draw that well, he was meticulous, and I realized he was a perfect candidate to handle color separations. In those days, almost every graphic piece needed a five-color mechanical separation. That was done with Rubylith, a red-plastic coating on acetate that was cut with a blade and peeled away. The work was exacting, tedious and took a great deal of my time. Andre took to it and I was elated. Now I could use pencils to quickly color a copy of the graphic and Andre would use that as a guide to place each color. Having him separating the colors was as good as doing it myself. It worked into a full time job for him for a few years.

I was finally getting some of the relief I needed. Before this time, each person I hired meant more management

JIMBO PHILLIPS: "I had a job at a fabric printing shop at the time and had only worked there a few months, when my dad told me he was starting an art studio for NHS in the house next door. It sounded really cool. My dad and I have always had a close relationship, but I would sometimes have a hard time when I worked for him, because he would sometimes ride me like dads do. But I couldn't pass up this great opportunity and my other job blew, so I quit and he hired me on as an apprentice in the art studio. Working for my dad turned out to be really great though. He would ride me but it was good because it pushed my level really

and training, no matter how much talent they displayed. Taking interviews was tough, because I wanted only artists who skateboarded and I had a limited budget. There were plenty of applicants and I was trying to guard against taking talent that needed too much developing, and too much time choosing. As it turned out, if they could draw anything at all I hired them just to get on with it. Most of them took up the challenge and starting with their first assignment of scrubbing the permanently brown-stained toilet. If they made it through that test I knew they were moldable. Most of them grew skills with amazing speed. As the workload grew heavier, I kept adding studio artists, including Danny Wenger who

by PHILLIPS

Jim helps Andreas Gingofer with an assignment while Jimbo works on the Natas Kitten design. (Below) 1989 studio group photo, Keith Meek, Hermel Mayang, Dolly Phillips, Jim Phillips, Andreas Ginghofer, John Munnerlyn.

Photos: Jim Raun-Byberg

lived across the street. He refused to scrub the toilet but his dad sent him right back over to do it. I took on Eric Cardinale and a kid named Chad, who lived in the neighborhood. Location was a factor because most of these kids didn't drive yet. Josh Evenson was Big John's son and he had showed some spunk with cartooning, so I brought him in. Joe Staley's mom came over and pleaded with us to take him; he had some definite talent drawing robots with guns. Hermel Mayang came in, Kevin Marburg, and John Munnerlyn. Keith Meek got booted off the NHS assembly line and wanted to come over to the studio, which the studio artists liked because he could give us the pro-rider perspective. Dolly assumed some of the clerical work in the studio, along with the Santa Cruz product catalogs and the typesetting for our ads that she had been doing all along.

DOLLY PHIL-LIPS: "Working on the catalogs was a good way for me to see first-hand, the art foaming up next door. The studio was a hotbed of ideas and off-the-wall antics, but at the same time the boys were very serious about doing a good job. Jimmy was masterful at keeping them on track and enthused."

Santa Cruz pro skaters came to the studio when it came time for their new graphics. I encouraged their ideas and always did my best to stoke them. In an effort to create the best graphic possible, I often tried to direct them to the better part of their idea, or tweak it somehow to help create a successful graphic. After discussing their graphics, the pros usually went out front for a skate jam with the studio guys at break time. The pro skating sessions definitely inspired their work and kept them tuned in.

Eventually, I had enough workers that I felt some relief from the pressure. I was very happy that we were able to handle the load. It was a dream come true .As a kid, I had looked at photos of Disney Studios with artists standing out front and wished I was one of them. Now I ran my own studio, although it was part of a larger entity. At the weekly office meeting at the factory, it was suggested that the studio have a manager. I wasn't thrilled with the idea of a newbie stepping in and trying to run everything. I already had my hands full, and wasn't looking forward to training someone in the details of everything I did. I remembered my days at Tracy's Fiberglas Works, my first studio art job, where Jim Raun-Byberg was art director, so I suggested him. Byberg was available and he came in as studio manager. Not knowing how to phase him in, and get going on a project, I put him to work enclosing the back porch for his office. The artists had been overflowing into an old shed in back so I had Byberg build a large light table and a row of drawing tables along one wall. We called it Studio B. After his small office was built, I assigned Byberg to refurbishing Studio B, which, after a few weeks, glowed with shiny grey painted floors and crisp white walls. The neighbors across the street were remodeling their kitchen and had their old cabinets out in the street, so I

instructed the boys to carry them back to Studio B where Byberg nailed them in. I had him make a rolling table for projecting 35mm slides onto ad-boards. The temperature seemed to be cooler in Studio B than the front studio in summer. Some of the boys preferred to work out there where they could play their music as loud as they wanted.

One morning, the studio B workers came into the front studio complaining of a stench. Apparently, when Byberg replaced some of the Studio B floorboards, a possum had crawled in and died. The smell was awful and big flies were showing the way. We cut a hole and fished out a maggot-filled carcass. I told Lousy to remove the skull and clean it up for the studio skull collection. All the studio artists came out to watch Lousy whack on the head with a machete while sipping out of a can of Mountain Dew. The head came off amid flying maggots, and I told Lousy to boil it. I had some briquettes and set a can of water on an old BBQ rack, and he attended it while it slowly simmered and stunk up the neighborhood. Lousy scraped and cleaned the skull and we brought it in and placed it next to the skulls we use to model from for drawings; some human skulls, a mountain lion skull, one of a sea lion with skateboard wheels in the eye sockets, a steer, and a few others.

The next morning, Kevin came in and told me he brought another skull for the studio collection. We went out to Mojo's car and opened his trunk. There was a huge cow's head, with all the meat and no skin. It had a three inch hole drilled in the forehead, and the boys explained how they had been to an SRL Laboratories show the night before, and how the cow's head got drilled in the show, along with other wildness. The boys somehow came into possession of the head and claimed it like a trophy. I had far more important issues to deal with, so I turned to Lousy and had him bury it in the back yard. There was a small ceremony and the studio artists made up a trophy-studded marker dedicated to the spirit of Elvis. Mojo drew a caricature of Lousy kissing the cow head, which they pinned up on the studio wall, and all was forgotten.

JIMBO PHILLIPS: "One night Lousy tells me about this show in San Francisco called SRL, Survival Research Laboratories. He said machines spewed fire and stuff and we needed to bring a cooler full of raw meat. We stopped at the butcher's, grab meat and beer, and headed to the city. We get there and pull up our chairs and our cooler. These machines come out and start destroying everything, belching fire and spewing

Phillips Studios photo 1988: (top row) Eric Cardinale, Andreas Ginghofer, Justin Forbes, John Munnerlyn, Jim & Dolly Phillips, (bottom) Josh Evenson, Hermel Mayang, Jimbo Phillips, Joe Staley.

Opposite page center: the boys ham it up at break, (top) Justin Forbes, Paul "Lousy" Hirsher, Jimbo Phillips, (lower left) Justin Forbes, (center) Jim Raun-Byberg, Kevin Marburg, Keith Meek, Andreas Ginghofer, Jimbo Phillips, (bottom) Jimbo catches air off the studio ramp. Illustrations by the studio artists, photos by Mojo.

John Munnerlyn

Keith Meek uses the copy machine in the studio kitchen. Original sketches are pinned on the wall for Bullet, Roskopp, and Speed Wheels. Also visible is the studio fridge, two sections of the art reference book library, and the back porch studio.

Studio Refrigerator

The studio skull collection was used for modeling and ads. It included human, human fetus, sea lion with wheels in the sockets, oppossum, bob-cat, steer, deer, and cow skulls, a whale vertibre, some miscellaneous bones, a tribal blowgun, and a tribute photo to Robert Williams.

photo: Mojo

PHILLIPS

STUDIO B

Photos courtesy of John Munnerlyn.

Hermel Mayang works on a wheel graphic on the Studio B light table.

Byberg looks for a spot to hang an old skate on one of the Studio B walls.

Rosie

Jim pauses for a photo in front of Studio B, at Phillips Studios.

John Munnerlyn, Keith Meek, Jim Raun-By-berg, Kevin Marburg, Andreas Ginghofer, Jimbo Phillips, Jim Phillips, pose in front of Byberg's office at Phillips Studios, 1989.

Below right,, the fabled Cowhead hangs under the studio back window. On the right, the Cowhead grave and monument, light reflected with mirror. Photos: Byberg.

COW HEAD

They chanted, "Cow head, cow head," as they drummed to the beat on the backyard tables and the old surfboards that leaned on the fence. Lousy dug deeper. I had a video camera and recorded what became known in close circles as "the Cow Head Video". I was enjoying the level of energy that the artists all had and knew it was inspirational for them, and sort of a reward for the long hours, hard work, and my exacting standards.

The video tape showed Lousy digging and getting closer to the cow head. He abandons the shovel as the studio artists chant, "Hand-dig, hand dig!" Soon, he's seen brushing some worms off and carefully pulling the large skull out. The crowd went wild. He cleaned it, hosing off the skull and working with what was referred to as his "toothbrush". Everyone grabbed their noses when he used a barbeque fork to clean out the eye sockets, of what was compared by Byberg to Rondele' cheese. Lousy got it fairly clean, and assumed the classic pose that was by now famous, after hanging in the studio for six months (Lousy, holding the cow head, other hand in his pants saying "I love you" while kissing it). There was no misinterpreting a drawing like that, so Lousy gained legendary status at the studio that day for action above and beyond the call of duty. I think the main office saw it as a goof off.

JIMBO: "The ultimate project was to do a deck graphic. Stickers and t-shirts were cool, but a deck graphic was the pinnacle. I eventually worked up to doing about seven or eight decks during this stint. I loved that job! There were some other cool guys who worked at the studio who I got along with and we had some great times.

grinded meat. So lousy whips open the cooler and starts throwing meat at the machines. I start laughing and throwing some and it goes into the grinder and spits out on the audience, it was gross. Lousy brings home one of the skulls from the show, fresh from the slaughterhouse, with eyes and tongue still intact and a huge hole in the forehead where a machine had drilled and burned into it from the show. He buried it in the backyard and dug it up a few months later, cleaned it, and added it to the studio skull collection. So Lousy!"

About six months later, a consensus formed among the artists that it was time to dig up the cow head. I bestowed the honor to Lousy for exhuming the thing. The studio artists were all stoked and decided that the final outcome should be for Lousy to pose like Mojo's caricature and kiss it. Lousy accepted his assignment with dignity. I handed him some shovels and he went to work digging. Of course the artists were all out there cheering and brought out a boom box with raging punk rock music.

JIMBO: One summer I took a road trip with a few of the guys (Justin, Mojo and Lousy), to see a Robert Williams exhibit in Los Angeles. We piled in Lousy's van and drove south, stopping to skate any and every spot we knew or saw. We skated some classic spots, like Venice High, Downtown L.A. and many others. There were no skate parks at this time so all spots were street, except ramps and backyard pools. We made it to the art show and it was cool, large full color paintings of weird monsters and hot chicks burned into our retinas. We had a great trip and came back so inspired!

While my studio artists worked away diligently, I would make rounds to answer their questions. There was always somebody needing help and my knee went out for a week from excessive rotating around in circles. Despite the hardships, it was one of my deepest pleasures to work with these raw young artists and see them grow artistically, to reach and excel under my tutelage. I was proud of the studio output and the achievement of a decent and consistent quality level. I was also encouraged about finally having the

ROAD TRIP

Robert Williams

Justin snapped this shot of Jimbo, Lousy and Mojo oustside the La Luz de Jesus gallery, on a road trip to Southern California to see a Robert Williams exhibit.

Lousy ponders the content in one of Robert Williams' original paintings.

Photos courtesy of John Munnerlyn.

SKATEBOARDING — ONLY — NO PEDESTRIANS, BIKES CARS, OR SCOOTERS

SKATEBOARD RIDING IS PROHIBITED

SKATEBOARDING — ONLY — NO PEDESTRIANS, BIKES CARS OR SCOOTERS

L.A.U.S.D.

NO

SKATEBOARDING — ONLY — NO PEDESTRIANS, B CARS, OR SCOOTE

Lousy and Justin post the new rules around L.A.   Photo: Mojo

NOR CAL'S ONLY WAVE CULTURE MAGAZINE

LOCAL
For the sea borne Magazine

Jimbo

ability to keep ahead of the bombardment of projects.

One day in 1989, I got the word that I would have to move the studio into the new cannery building. I was told that we would henceforth be separated from the accounting department by a long glass window. I panicked and dug in my heels. I couldn't see keeping the creative spirit alive while working in plain view of the bean counters that would be watching our every move. I used my own home studio at no charge for fifteen years and thought I deserved to stay put. I worked hard to build the studio next door and mad it work. Subsequently, I was fired. But they asked me to stay on for the next year while they built offices at the cannery, and then I'd be fired. It was half my pay but I accepted, just to keep going. After the year was over, I asked to stay, that I would be willing to move, but that was denied. It was very sad for me to see all my

VIdeo

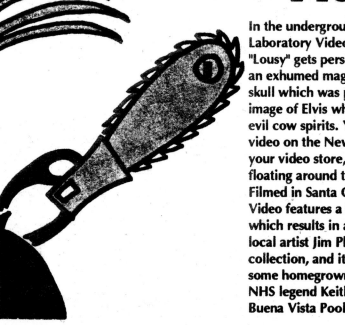

In the underground Phillips Laboratory Video, "Cowhead", "Lousy" gets personal with Friend, an exhumed maggot infested heifer skull which was protected by an image of Elvis which wards away evil cow spirits. You wont find this video on the New Arrivals shelf of your video store, but it's been floating around town for a while. Filmed in Santa Cruz, Cowhead Video features a bizarre ritual which results in a new addition to local artist Jim Phillips skull collection, and it also highlights some homegrown pool skating of NHS legend Keith Meek at the Buena Vista Pool.

artists leave. To make matters worse, Dolly and Jimbo were let go as well; Merry Christmas. I bought some of the tables and equipment, and continued using the studio for art. Now it was really my own studio but I didn't have a stable of artists working day and night. I was trying to unwind, but I was soon diagnosed with hypertension after half my face became temporarily paralyzed. I was dangerously stressed out. Obviously it was the best thing for me to be let go at that time. I believe my work would have consumed me.

IT WAS JUST ANOTHER DAY IN MY LIFE, *UNTIL* I RECEIVED A LETTER FROM ED McMAHON... UNTIL I STARTED USING DRY IDEA...BUT *MAINLY* UNTIL MY EDITOR ORDERED ME TO DRAW A CARTOON FEATURE STORY ABOUT...

I WANT THE QUINTESSENTIAL SKATEBOARD FEATURE ON MY DESK TOMORROW A.M. FARB! AND OH YES, PUT SOME RESEARCH INTO IT.. OR *YOU'RE FIRED!*

GULP!

GETTA *MOVE* ON FARB!

SLAM

GOSH, HOW CAN I DRAW SKATE STORIES WHEN I'VE NEVER EVEN *TRIED* IT! I'LL HAVE TO GET A *SKATEBOARD* TO REALLY GET INTO THIS... ..NOW WHERE DID I SEE THAT SKATE SHOP? HMMM...

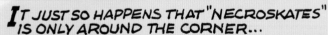

IT JUST SO HAPPENS THAT "NECROSKATES" IS ONLY AROUND THE CORNER...

Heh heh Come in, I have things of need to you --Farb!

You will take this one, you know it is a death trap... But you will take it won't you? heh, heh heh!

I'LL TAKE IT!

NEXT MORNING,

HMMM...

OOPS!

YOW!

In 1991 I got well, went back to surfing, and was doing some surf art (the Hand Wave), while enjoying my now-abundant free time. I attended the 1991 Action Sports trade show in San Diego trying to dig up some jobs. There I met Roy Gonzales and Salvador Paskowitz who showed me some proofs of their upcoming premiere issue of Surf Crazed Comics. It was their color work, especially the red-to-yellow blends in the flames of Roy's "Aloha from Hell" two-page spread he colored in Photoshop that sold me on color computers. And it was the right time, because digital output for production was becoming state of the art. Dolly had used a computer for years as a typesetting tool, ever since the Mac came out in '85. We used a black and white laser printer that made nice type, but color output had not been good enough to pay the high costs. Suddenly, it became a vital tool that was essential for art. My primary motivation to own a color Mac was for coloring my pen and ink drawings, but it became so much more than that. The computer was so new at this time that it gave me a business edge. This lead to my long series of San Francisco rock posters, reviving an art form that I had left behind more than a decade before. I made posters for Bill Graham Presents Fillmore, became Family Dog Productions' art director, and hunted down some of San Francisco's most famous rock graphic artists to make posters. Attending these shows, meeting people and famous musicians at the concert halls, and partying until late in the city was a cool way for an old washed-up skateboard artist to go to pasture.

HMMM...

LOOKS LIKE ONE OF MY WHEELS!

LOOKS LIKE ONE OF MY TRUCKS! HMMM..

LOOKS LIKE...

CRASH

YOU DIDN'T DO A VERY GOOD JOB ON THE SKATE BOARD STORY, FARB!

KINDA SLOPPY IF YOU ASK ME, FARB!

YEA, WELL IT'S HARD WITH A SKATEBOARD IN YOUR MOUTH!

FIN

158

Catalog page featuring the work of Jim Phillips, Jimbo Phillips, John Munnerlyn, Justin Forbes, Hermel Mayang, and a 6 year old neighbor kid named Brian, 1988.

TIPS FOR NEW SKATEBOARD OWNERS

SKATE SAFELY Take it slow and don't skate beyond your ability. Always wear safety gear (wrist guards are most important) and watch for traffic. Most motorists can't see you until it's too late, so keep your eyes open.

THEFT Skateboards get stolen very easily. Don't leave yours in the side-yard, backyard, garage, front porch, school locker, car or in front of a store. Keep your eyes on it or keep it under your feet.

WATER DAMAGE If you want your skateboard to last, *stay out of water!* It will rust your bearings, delaminate your deck, and destroy your bushings. Try your best to avoid it.

LUBRICATION Skateboards need no lubrication at all, if you *stay out of water!* The bearings are packed in a long lasting grease and stay well lubricated. Water will break down the grease and rust your bearings.

ADJUSTMENTS Trucks should be tightened or loosened to turn to your liking, but no other adjustments are needed. All the hardware is self locking and should stay snug, but check it once in awhile. Wheels should have a slight bit of "play", without being loose. An "elephant" skate wrench fits both the truck and wheel adjustment nuts.

MAINTENANCE Keep an eye on your nose guard, tail guard, rails, lapper, copers and truck suspension bushings and replace if worn out. Check your truck mounting hardware and T-bolts for looseness and tighten if needed.

WARRANTY/COVERAGE Make sure you receive, read, fill out and send in a Warranty Card. (Only Santa Cruz offers a warranty with every Santa Cruz deck.) This will protect you for 30 days if the board breaks from manufacturing defects. (See the Warranty Card for more details.)

 Most boards crack or break at the back truck holes. The main cause of this is improper foot placement when landing jumps. Using a Cell Block III on the backtruck helps prevent breakage, but landing jumps with both feet over the trucks is the best way to avoid this problem.

Justin Forbes

John Munnerlyn   Jimbo Phillips

Troy Stone

Don Hillsman

Brent Belle

Chris Elliman

Slimeball t-shirt, 1986.

Ubiquitous bumper sticker.

Dolly Phillips

LONGEST RAILSLIDE!

SKID MARX SLID THE ENTIRE B & O RAILROAD FROM CHICAGO TO LOS ANGELES NONSTOP. AND PULLED IT. TO FAKIE!

Justin

The SKATER WHO COULDN'T SKATE!

DARREL PISSAQUESKY OF DAYTON, OHIO WORE SKATEBOARD SHORTS AND T-SHIRTS DAILY. TALKED USING ALL THE SKATE LINGO AND RAD TERMS. BUT NEVER SKATED. ALTHOUGH HE ALWAYS HAD THE LATEST MODEL (IN MINT CONDITION)!

WAY RAD AWSOME DUDE JIBBER JABBER BLABBER OLLIE SPRAK BLAH BLAH BLAH...

TRY YODELING THIS!

Mojo

IN 1983

A HEALTHY CANADIAN GOOSE WAS FOUND WITH A RAIL THROUGH ITS NECK! THE GOOSE DISAPPEARED FOR 6 YEARS 'TIL IT WAS SPOTTED AT A LONGEST RAIL SLIDE CONTEST!

Hermel

SKATE RAMP TO OBLIVION!

THIS RAMP IN OBLIVION NEBRASKA IS REALLY NOTHING SPECIAL!

Justin

THE SKATER WHO ONLY PHOTOGRAPHS SPECTATORS. IN FACT. NO ONE HAS EVER SEEN THIS MAN'S FACE ... IN FACT. HIS CAMERA IS BOLTED TO HIS FACE!

Jim

KURTIS FORSKIN OF SHMEGVILLE KENTUCKY WAS PULLED OVER ON HIS SKATE BY A LOCAL POLICEMAN

AND WAS **COMMENDED** ON HIS SKATING! AND ACTUALLY TOLD TO KEEP UP THE GOOD WORK!

Jimbo

THE EARTH IS NOT ROUND!

NOR IS IT PEAR SHAPED! IN FACT. IT RESEMBLES MORE OF A TRAPEZOIDAL MOBIUS PARALLELAGRAM!

PHILLIPS STUDIOS

Jimbo

Ripper's— Believe It or Bail!

Featured in Cracked Magazine

SKATEBOARD JEWELRY!

WHEN A BRAZIL BOUND SKATACURB SHIPMENT WASHED UP ON THEIR SHORES, SOUTH AMERICAN LOCAL TRIBES MEN REGARDED IT AS MYSTIC MOJO JEWELRY AND ADORNED THEMSELVES WITH SKATEBOARD ACCESSORIES! YET THEY REFUSE TO ASSEMBLE A SKATE!

Justin

SOON TO BE EXTINCT!

THE MOST ENDANGERED REPTILE "THE KNEE-CAP TURTLE" FOUND ONLY IN THE DEEPEST PARTS OF THE AMAZON JUNGLE!

THE TURTLE IS USED BY NATIVES AS **KNEE PADS.** BOWLS. HATS. CUPS. BRAS. ATHLETIC SUPPORTERS. MASKS. SHOVELS. HOOD-ORNAMENTS. JELLO MOLDS...ETC.!!!

Hermel

THE SKATEBOARD GRAPHIC

THAT **DIDN'T** OFFEND PARENTS!

IN FACT. THIS FAMILY IN JOCKSTON. U.S.A. ACTUALLY YANKED THEIR YOUNG SON **OFF** THE BASEBALL TEAM AND **FORCED HIM** TO PURSUE SKATING!

Justin

13 YEAR OLD BOY GETS ELECTRIC CHAIR FOR SKATING DOWN SIDEWALK!

HOWEVER HE DID KILL SEVEN **PEOPLE** WHILE SKATING DOWN THAT SIDEWALK!!!

THE SKATEBOARD ARTISTS WHO WOULDN'T GIVE UP!

NO MATTER HOW INSIPID THE JOKES. THESE **DEMENTED** CARTOONISTS KEPT CRANKIN' 'EM OUT!

Justin

NO ELVIS?
DURING THE MONTH OF JANUARY. 1989. THERE WERE ABSOLUTELY **NO ELVIS** SIGHTINGS WORLD WIDE!

Justin

Jimbo

PHILLIPS STUDIOS
FEATURED IN CRACKED MAGAZINE NO 250

SKATA CURB

MOTORIZED SKATEBOARD

Do zero to 60 mph in 5 seconds!

Hydro V8

Turbo charged

Top fuel class, fully equiped w/turbo hemi-injected V8! Plus Hydromatic transmission, Eight ball gear shift & big foot gas pedal all included.(Please specify goofy foot or regular! $999.00

STOP SKATE HARASSMENT

Detects with **FUZZ BUSTER** Police presence within 5000 ft

ONLY $975.00 CHEAP

WACKY BEARINGS

Spread some of these wobbly wheel bearings around & eliminate some competition Each....$5.75

KRUEGER SKATE GLOVES

comes with leather padded palm and razor sharp super grip finger tips. No one will snake you again......$49.95

BRAIN WORMS FUN!

Turn your friends into instant vegetables with these wiggling wonders! Just sprinkle some **larve** into their helmets and watch the **fun** begin!Your friends will be sure to sketch their next run when these nibblin' parasites penetrate their grey matter! You will have the skate spots all to yourself while your friends sit and drool! 1 dz. worms.....$1.99

NEW! OLLIE MASTER

155mm $115.95
166mm $135.95

OLLIEMASTER
You'll be king of the block!!! Effortlessly launch into the Natas realm.

GLASS TRUCKS

Looks like metal but wait 'til they hit the coping!

Pair only $18.99

JAMES BOND OIL SLICK Spreader

Attaches to tail in seconds, works great for evading police, bullies, parents and girl friend. Specify spray or squirt. On Sale at only $89.95

MOWER TRUCKS

SLASH THE GRASS

FUN!

This handy device. Each......$39.95
Option Grass Catcher.........$12.95

5000 VORACIOUS TERMITES

The fun starts when you release these hungry huge African Termites under that ramp that you can't use, yours for only $3.95 BUG YOUR FRIENDS

TOP 40 SKATE HITS Volume II

All the great skate hits are in Volume II, including: James Brown Poppa's Gotta Brand New Board & I Skate Good, Wilson Picket Skate 'til the Midnght Hour, Patsy Cline Skating After Midnight, Led Zeppelin Stair Rail to Heaven, Carl Perkins Blue Suede Converse, Madonna Like a Betty, The Clash Should I Skate or Should I Go?, The Who Won't Get Chapped Again, The Beatles McTwist & Shout, Willie Nelson You Were Always on My Grind, Steppenwolf Born to Be Rad, Lou Reed Skate on the Wild Side, Arlo Guthrie Alice's Skatepark, Jan & Dean Skate City, Creedance ClearWater Revival Betty Q, Micheal Jackson Whack It, Everly Brothers Skate Up Little Suzie, Four Tops Back Wheels in Motion, more, $9.95

EXPLODING SKID PLATE VIET NAM STYLE HOO! HAH!

The fun starts when your friends unwittingly try these old surplus Viet Cong field mines, guaranteed to maim. Discount price........$45.00

RECTUM SKATE SHORTS

Be COOL?

With internal rectal thermometer, be the hottest or the coolest! Only $72.00

WHOOPIE COPERS!

BRAP WHOOPIE

FART FLAPPERS - When you grind lappers, blast the crowd and relish in the joy.1 set..............$19.95

Authentic HUMAN SKULL. This freshly dug up piece will add charm to your room. Will also add charming fresh dug up aroma to your room. $50

FAKE FAKE DOG POOP

Have the last laugh. Your friends will skate into it thinking it's fake, but **it's real!** $14.95 Each

REAL Authentic smelling **DINGLE BALLS** for a **real** hair ball ride! Clings to any surface. $5.00
Simulated mink **FUR BALLS**. Quiet, smooth and sensuous. Betties love it when you skate on their bodies w/ these $10

SKATANIC VOICES

by Salmon Rushtodie you'll be in a rush to die too when you buy this book! You'll hear voices ordering your own death after reading this book criticizing Ayotollah's skating abilities. $29.95

SLIMEBALL GUM

They'll never get the taste out of their mouths after you offer some of this hilarious gum. 97A Extra Hot chili pepper. Chief Proudoh won't even be able to stand it. 95A Formaldehyde Taste, gets rid of messy teeth. 92. Putrification Flavor. Explodes in your mouth leaving a burnt flesh taste Now only .... 75¢ a pac

FOAM RUBBER BUSHINGS

Slip these spongy soft rubber bushings into the inventory at your local shop & watch the fun Each only now 29¢

SKATE SWEAT

One can $12.95

Authentic kneepad stench Impress the chicks. They'll think you've been sessioning.

E-rector

Re-Cap Jock Strap great for crotch endangering hand rail bails. Comes in two different styles for males & females $8.95 ea or 2 for $30

NOSE GUARDS

Use type A Guard to protect the nose of your board B when you run into stuff. Use type B when you run into the stuff's owner. $3.95 per nose

SCREAMING BIRD

T-shirts, decals, keychain, banners, pins, sweats, underwear, lingerie, socks, earrings, sunglasses, body lotion, shoe laces, switchblade knives, condoms. 49¢ ea. Life size vibrating latex screaming bird $24.95.Sorry, no wheels.

DR. LOUIE'S LOBOTOMY DRILL

New Improved

Are you plagued by the pressure and stress of modern life? **THEN VENTILATE YOUR BRAIN!** Lost your job? Landlord says the rent is late? Police harass you for skating? Girlfriend left you for the local football team? **Solve these problems and more INSTANTLY!** Includes 1/2" dia. drill bit and 2" dia. hole saw for those really bad days.. $19.99

Everybody 'll be "Skatin' USA" after you slap some of these SKATEBOARDING ONLY signs on top of all those NO SKATEBOARDING signs at the mall. Box of 3000 for $3.50 each.

M60 MACHINE GUN

60 MM 550 ROUNDS PER MINUTE BELT FED

Put Firepower where you need it with this baby. M-60 general purpose machine gun. Mom leaning on you to clean your room? Don't get mad, get even. A steal at only..........................$1560.00 each

M-115 203mm HOWITZER only $5000.00 each

FUN!

The fun starts when you roll up to the local skate bowl armed with your very own 203mm Howitzer Artillery Cannon. Imagine the surprised look of the guys running around with puny AK47 assault rifles.

CASTRADO SCIENTIFIC EMASCULATOR FAST

Retain that youthful choirboy voice......... $3.95

SKATE BETTY CHASTITY BELT

You traveling pros won't have to worry about your girl's virtue while you're on tour with this NEW NON Chauvo-Pig Model all metal chastity belt with bear trap snap action! Includes padlock. Each $35.00

ELECTRO SHOCK TREATMENT HELMET

No more expensive psychotherapy with this item.

AC Model $49.95
DC model $149.95

INSTA BETTY

Inflatable date, never worry about picking up on girls again. This perfect 36-22-34 blondie will go with you everywhere and never complains. Will sit happily for hours on end while you skate. SAFE SEX- No prob.No birth control required. Plastic BETTY..$39.95

LIVE grenades!

Famous pineapple fragmentation device of WWII. Don't take any more lip from the anti-skate faction. A REAL BLAST!

Low Riders BUMP!

Cruise on up to the next halfpipe session thumpin' and bumpin'.
Custom board...............$250.00

ICE TRACK WHEEL

Tired of falling on your ice? Snow on your ramp bumming your day? TRY NEW ICE TRACK WHEELS for skating tobbogans or just for that extra grip. $8.99

$12.95 SKATE GUITAR HOO-HAH!

Combo of Deck and Axe will create sounds that will make people want to axe your deck and maybe even you!!! $12.95

FLY IN THE DRINK JOKE HOO HAH!

Everyone will think its the old fly in the cube, but these disgusting babies are real. 95¢
Horse Fly........$2.35

ACME DELUXE SLIMEBALL ACCELERATOR

This baby packs a whallop. 1200 meter range, 20 megaton payload $32,000.00 FOB
*Dealer prep, tax and license included with each.

20 MEGATO

SANTA MONICA AIRBOARDS

120 MPH

Get air for hours on this amazing device. Commuters save hours of traffic gridlock air into the stratosph check out the ozone! It amazing we don't even k how it works!.Only $76
Santa Monica Parachu
Due to design flaws in rent in Santa Monica boards, you really should h one of these, too. Only $29

THE SKATER'S BIBLE

NO WANNABE SHOULD BE WITHOUT IT!
POSEUR'S ENCYCLOPEDIA OF SKATE TERMS

Now you can sound like s skater without ever skating! Keep abreast of the latest skate lingo w/this trusty tome. Over 15,000 entries including: Shocka, spracka, soochie, vermin, squalor, dew it, cruncher, hoedad, sporble, hango-bo-dango, crackle-a-spackle, phulu, jah no, hoo haa, meyawn cracken dew, ska biff, hectic hemis, wankin, lagging, en homygrity, splorch, bonglord, spalkink, chortle, slither, sechwan beaver, tie die guac squirt, muddy henshian bung, cheesy sac, snat, whips, drippy chicklets, squareme, flowage, snivel, hubba, mego, poo doggy style, jizzum, loins, whadish, bowo, nardlipe, slick, fick, crappy broski, honky, cuffs, sixer, skaboosh, snared, ragging, slerbo. $69.9

SKATA CURB

I don't want any of this garbage but I want t send plenty of money anyway! I realize I won be receiving any thing but here's my addres for your sucker list.
Name
Address ___ City ___ Zip
Bank Acct # ___
Net Worth ___ ATM Code ___
Safe Deposit # ___
Girl friend's name & phone ___
If we are not absolutely thrilled with your mone we will provide a full refund!

PHILLIPS ST

SKATA CURB

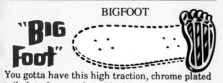

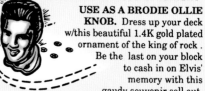
PHILLIPS STUDIOS

The Tortoise and Hare drawing was the splash panel for my 1989 update of Aesop's fable, to be the first page of Road Rash No 2. The Comic was my pet project and I wanted it to be the best possible. A tall order considering the responsibility that I was shouldering at Phillips Studios, training a team of young skater-artists while keeping up with graphics and ads for a forty million dollar bottom line at Santa Cruz. The comic floated on the back burner, and I worked on it at night. Eventually, I set one of my studio artists, Hermel Mayang, to sketch out the rest of the story which revolved around a great challenge between the Tortoise and Hare, and their skateboard race through the city to the finish line, as they are distracted in various ways making their way through the city, while plotting against each other. I had Hermel redraw plenty of the panels, but he plugged away faithfully and I thought he did an excellent job. I didn't think his skills were polished enough for inking, so I put him onto other projects, and tried to get enough spare time to ink the story myself. The head office was throwing jobs at me left and right with short deadlines. It was like working in a tornado. But the comic stayed in the back of my mind, as I reasoned, skateboarders and comic book readers fall into the same age group. I kept trying to figure out

how to keep it going, so I began to look at my freelance file. The office forwarded inquiries and art samples from artists from around the country. It was complicated to work with free-lance artists, but I was impressed with an artist from Georgia, Don Hillsman and called him.. Around that time, I was let go. This half finished drawing was in one of the piles of art leftover. The rest of the inked story was lost in the shuffle. What this unique piece of art provides is an anatomy of my technique at the time. A moment frozen in time. What you see is a half inked page. You can see the blue-line drawing on the un-inked lower portion. Blue is non-repro, or non-reproducible with a stat camera. A close look will show much about the technique, such as the inking sequence. See how the key lines are developed on a separate plane. The car in the foreground has been outlined. The characters have been inked and detailed. Then the background elements are drawn in the same way; outline, then shading and texture. Opposite page: the pencil sketch of this panel. Not much can be said about pencil sketches, except that this first stage happens in a matter of minutes, rather than the long hours of inking a blue line version. And I think it is the purest expression of the art, spontaneous and free. After sketching, the work is carefully labored over, detailed, reshaped and refined. below is the second plot-unfolding panel of the story, in the same unfinished state.

The hood of Dolly's '67 Mustang was the scene of a sticker photo-shoot for the catalog.

Photo: Jim Byberg.

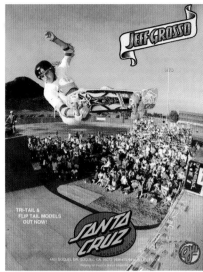

Here's a few of the Santa Cruz ads which appeared in various magazines.

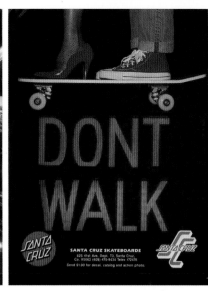

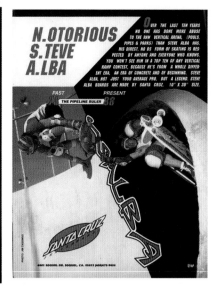

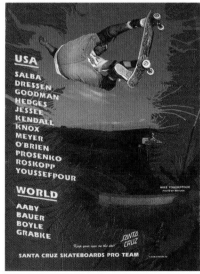

NEW SHAPES • GRAPHICS • TATOO

JASON large 10.125" X 31.0"
JASON small 10.0" X 30.0"
'CRUZ MISSILE CONCAVE'
CLEAN LEG INK

SANTA CRUZ

DEATH

A CURE ALL

...SOME OF THE WHEEL ADS.

DEATH

IN THE AIR

DEATH

IS IT NO SECRET

MAX SPEED-CUTTING STREET EDGE
BULLETS NEW WAR PAINT
97A BROKEN CHURCH GLASS
NEW- 66 MM BULLET W/WAR PAINT

BULLET

SPEED WHEELS SANTA CRUZ

Wheels of Fire
Takin' You Higher

OJII SPEED WHEELS SANTA CRUZ

1986

OJII Elites

OJII

bullet

MUSTARD GAS

"Slide 'em!" "They blaze!" "They rule!" "Roll 'em!" "The fastest!"
"No doubt!"
"More control!"
"Da' kine slides!"
"Way' air"

BULLET

OJ II 97A

SLIME BALLS

"Fast wheels
relieve excess
reality"

DOTS = WHEEL BITE DESIGN

CATCH FREE RADIUS   TOTAL FLOW DUAL RADIUS
ANTI-KNUCKLE BURNS

BIG BALLS
BY: SLIMEBALL
65mm
364mmM/HR

ON COMMAND SLIDE   FASTER THAN HELL

DOES THIS SORE LOOK INFECTED?

SPEED WHEELS SANTA CRUZ

408 475 9434

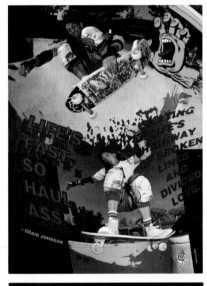

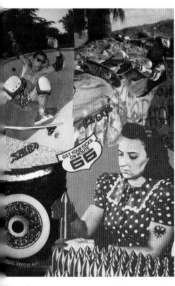

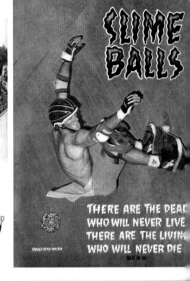

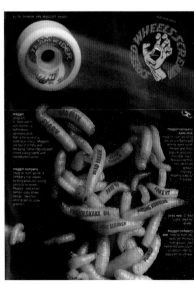

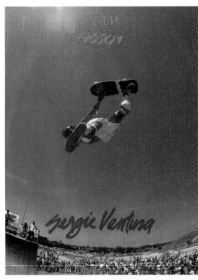

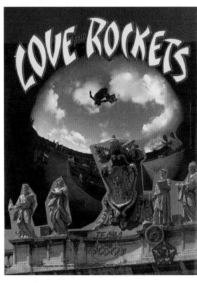

...some of the Hosoi ads.

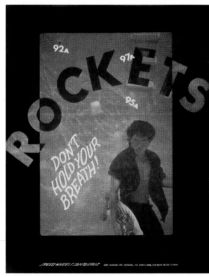

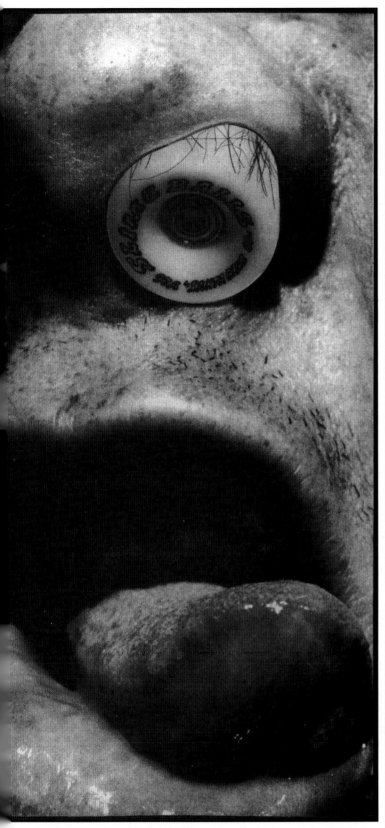

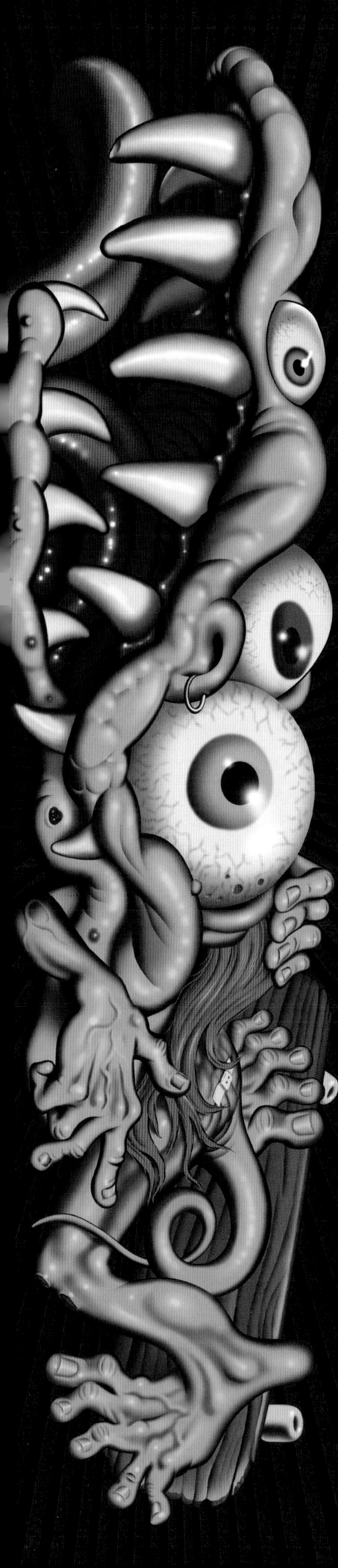

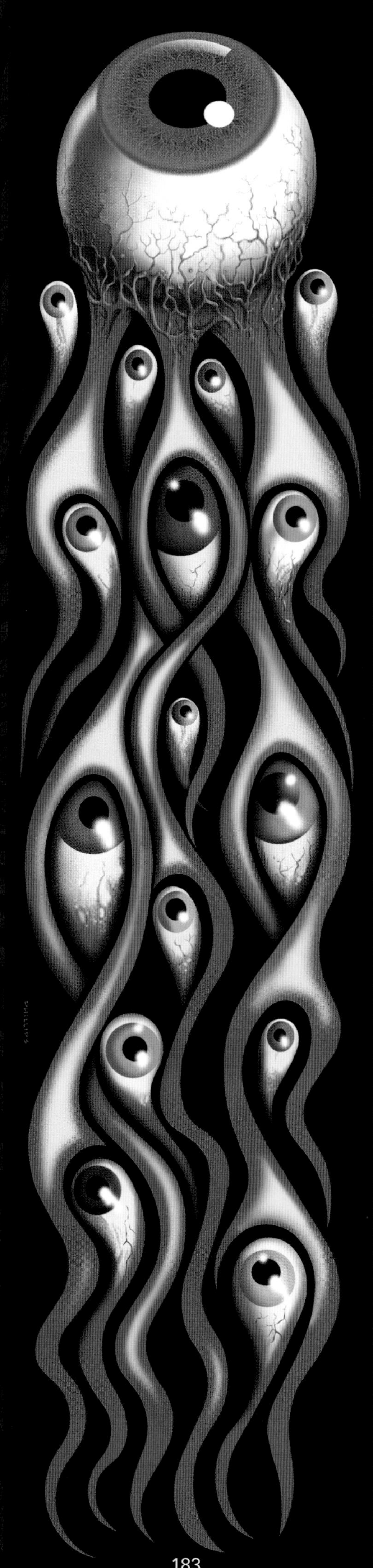

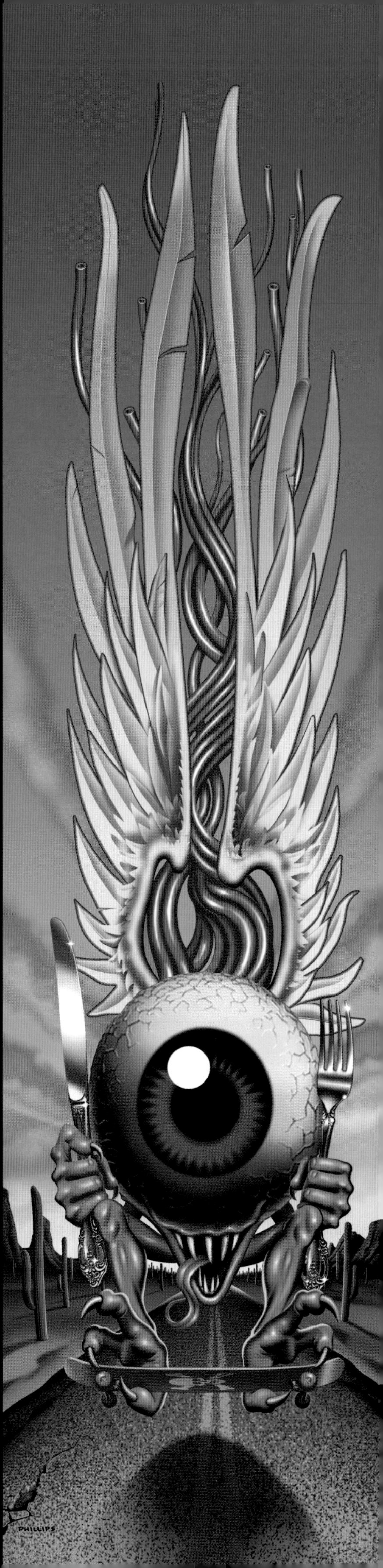

Jim and Jimbo pose for Deckarama publicity photos.

Jim's 2005 hand painted board for
Dogtown skateboard exhibit
and benefit auction.

PACK YOUR TRASH

GEEK
GEEK SKATE BOARDS

PACK YOUR TRASH .COM

PLEASURE POINT NIGHT FIGHTERS

MATT FRENCH: "I'll have to admit, it wasn't the easiest thing to begin a dialogue with someone I held in such high regard. As in any such situation, it helps to have something to break the ice...and I had this: A couple years before, when I was just beginning my career as an artist, I made it my mission to paint portraits of my heroes in the skateboard industry. I emailed a request to Jim for a photo to paint his portrait from, and he was glad to help me out. A few days later, I received an envelope of photos with my name and address hand-written by Jim on the envelope. At the same time, I told Jeff Kendall at NHS about my plan to paint Jim's portrait. He thought it sounded like a cool idea, and, at my request, gave me a Santa Cruz deck to paint Jim's portrait on. After painting Jim's portrait on the deck, I put some Independent 169 trucks on it (these were also from Jeff Kendall), and I rounded out the situation with a set of never-ridden OJ Combos wheels from the 80s. These were one of the wheels that featured Jim's screaming hand art. Upon completion, I gave the portrait skateboard to Jim, to show my appreciation. So when I started calling him, I had something to break the ice in that first conversation. After that, things just got ridiculous. Jim has done so many graphics that coming up with a truly new concept is like a quest for the unattainable grail. It's a love-hate, laughter-frustration, with the hope that out of it all, will be born a good concept with good art. I've never been so pissed, or laughed so hard in my life, as with my conversations with Jim. Every last bit of it has been fun though, and I've really learned a lot about what it takes to make a good graphic."

Matt painted a portrait of Jim on this deck (left), as part of the Volcom Featured Artist show at the Volcom Store in Los Angeles, 2006.

In 2006, Matt French of Lynden, Washington, came into my life. He gained my confidence with his graphics skills; you can tell a lot by that. He was acting as art director for Pocket Pistols Skates based in Huntington Beach, California. Matt was also one of their team riders and he asked me to design his team model. I know I must have come off seeming crusty and disgusted with the industry, but he wore me down. He has a knack for calling art supply companies and talking them into sending free merchandise, so he called them again and had them send me stuff. I was flooded with paint, India-ink pens, brush pens, drawing paper, sketchbooks, and ink. He even convinced the great folks at Microtek to send me a top-of-the-line ScanMaker 1000XL with 18-inch scanner bed, which I soon realized was crucial to creating the book. Matt also has a knack for coaching young skaters and is connected with a lot of old-school skaters. He put out the call that I was working on a book and I was again flooded, with old skateboards and wheels bearing my artwork from all around the country. Matt and I spend a lot of time talking about art. We frequently shoot sketches back and forth by email, and often crack each other up with groaners and worse. Matt has a great attitude, and our relationship brought back the spirit of studio days that I enjoyed at Phillips Studios, with today's Internet making such a thing possible.

I was working on a Model A pickup truck, which was in disassembly in my garage, when Matt first called. He wanted a design for his personal Pocket Pistols' team-rider deck, and I was happy to keep working with wrenches. He suggested that we keep things simple and base the graphic on one of his favorite comic panels of mine involving a character named Farb. Matt even provided a rough sketch that had his name coming out in barf. I accepted the job and before long it sank in that it was my first deck graphic on a modern "popsicle" shaped skateboard deck, and also my first deck graphic since I had left Santa Cruz more than fifteen years before. They were also my first decks with computer assistance. Doing color separations for decks by computer is far superior to old-world techniques. The best part for an artist is that you can see the actual colors you are using, instead of red film or black ink separations where you must imagine the color combination effects.

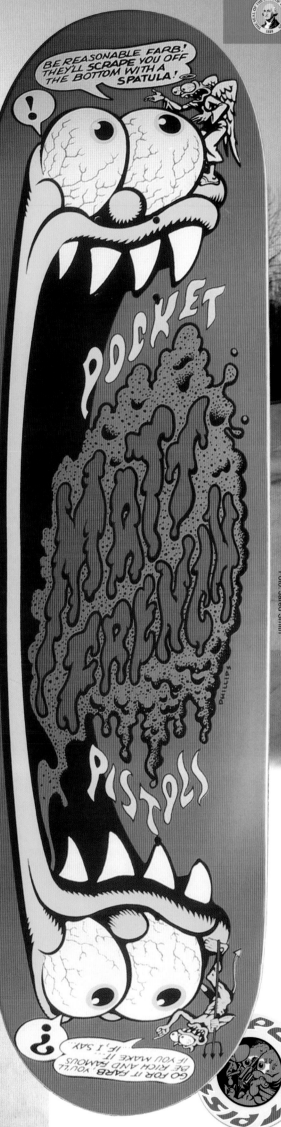

MATT FRENCH: "This whole series of conversations was so unreal to me, that I hardly remember all that was said. It's like I blacked out from disbelief. What I saw when these decks arrived and I opened the box, was a deck graphic of a guy with green eyes & skin tone like me, wrestling with his fear, to the point of puking. And like the seers of ages past, I read the puke, and there was my name!"

Pretty soon Matt was hounding me for another deck and asked what might be in my archives that we could use. I suggested what I had dubbed "Screaming Deck", using just the mouth from Screaming Hand. The famous hand logo had been dead for some years and I was still trying do avoid doing a custom design. Screaming Hand was never actually printed on a skateboard deck during my tenure, as it was a logo for wheels. Pocket Pistols' owner Barrett "Chicken" Deck was stoked to produce the Screaming Deck, and his quality printing helped make me a believer in his operation. Chicken is one of those skaters who never tapered off over years of skating. He's a slalom champion as well as one of the premier screen deck printers in skateboarding today.

"Radzilla" was Matt's name for another deck we did using my Psychotic Skater 9page 190). Originally the art was second in a line of skateboard decks for Psychotic Wheels. The deck line was canned in mid-production of the Psychotic Skater design, I presume in deference to the deck division. I was enthused to have the design finally used on a deck, after sitting in moth balls for twenty years.

MATT FRENCH: "One of the things I love about this graphic is how it resembles the classic cartoon situation where the timid little victim guy drinks the serum, grows to an enormous size, and gets the better of his tormentors. Kinda reminds me of Go Skate Day on June 21. I guess the more obvious thing would be the similarity to the classic gigantic Japanese monsters, of which Godzilla is the most widely known."

Foto: Jared Smith

Along the way, Matt came up with a job offer to collaborate on a large velvet day-glo poster for Volcom. I suggested doing a vole skating, and he came up with the Vole-UH-tile title, which I thought was quite funny. It sounded crazy but paid well and I liked working with Matt, so I went for it. We sent dozens of sketch ideas back and forth and talked for hours each day. We penciled in dozens of sight gags and puns, including a lot of tile jokes. We broke the design into sections to work alternately, and we broke each other up. We took turns inking our collective pencil sketches, sometimes me inking his sketches and him inking mine, all the while scanning, emailing and calling back and forth. Matt was able to cope with my picky standards and turned out work I was proud to be associated with.

MATT FRENCH: "When Jim and I first embarked on the Vol-UH-tile project, we both agreed to put our feelings and egos aside and do whatever it took, even if it was the physical or verbal ripping apart of each others' art to create a good graphic. I felt that there was no better venue for such a project than Volcom, and when they let Jim and I do whatever we wanted, Jim agreed. Over the couple weeks that followed, what transpired was, to this day, one of my favorite art projects ever."

Eventually I caved and started some new deck designs on a royalty basis, and there was enough interest in it for me get hung up on it. I flew some sketches past Matt and we were off and running with a new series. Around that time I got an email from a friend, German skater Claus Grabke, asking if I could do a deck for his Die Claus Grabke Retrospektive exhibition at the Stuttgart Skateboard Museum. It was amazing to get him in with Pocket Pistols, since he just won a German slalom race on a Pocket Pistols board. Claus is not only one of the best European skaters, but he has an antique clock collection so all of the decks I have done for him were about clocks. I conjured up a updated version H.G.Wells' Time Machine, where Time Traveler explores the history of skateboarding.

CLAUS GRABKE: "I was absolutely blown away by the "Time Machine". It's the best skateboard graphic ever! What an honor to work with Jim again after all these years!"

concrete wave
100% SKATEBOARDING

HE'S BACK!

AFTER A 15 YEAR HIATUS FROM THE SKATEBOARD INDUSTRY
THE LEGENDARY JIM PHILLIPS IS BACK!
LOOK FOR THE NEW PPS JIM PHILLIPS ARTIST SERIES COMING SOON!

Pocket Pistiol's magazine ad trumpets the news.

POCKETPISTOLSKATES.COM

RACER X

Jason
Mitchell
Racer X

PHILLIPS

189

This Psychotic deck graphic took more than 20 years to finally get on a deck. It was renamed Radzilla by Matt French.

SUPER RAT

PISTOLS POCKET

SUPER RAT.COM

SUPER RAT

SUPER RAT
PHILLIPS

SUPER RAT
PHILLIPS

Foto: Gerd Reiger

Claus Grabke
the Time Machine

FILMHAUS STUTTGART
(NAHE HAUPTBAHNHOF)
ZWEITES UNTERGESCHOSS
FRIEDRICHSTRASSE 23A
70174 STUTTGART

POCKET PISTOLS

Jim Phillips rides the Hand Wave
longboard, 2007. Photo: Dolly.

Makoto Nakashima

194

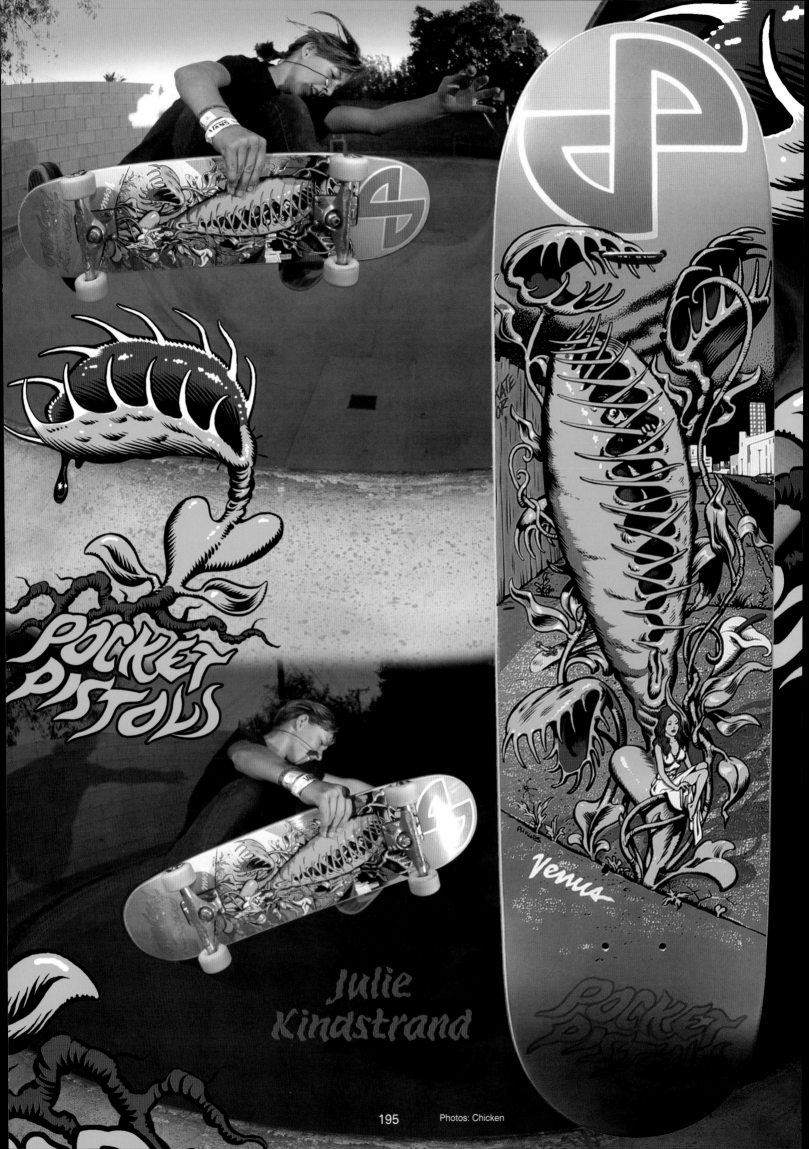

POCKET PISTOLS

Venus

Julie Kindstrand

Photos: Chicken

COLLABORATION
Phillips / French

Photo: Jared Smith

12 X 32.5

Photo: Rolan Baughan

The Pocket Pistols logo was previously a once-used Phillips fine art "chop" involving the initials: JP.

Photo: Arab

WWW.POCKETPISTOLSKATES.COM

SCREAMIN' INC.

SCREAMIN' INC.

198

Chris Hamrock

199

bone-hand

Tadayuki Kato

BEAMS
SURF + SKATE

Ryan Reyes

BEAMS
SURF + SKATE

Pocket Pistols

BEAMS
SURF + SKATE

Pocket Pistols

glow in the dark

Pocket Pistols

Photo: Chicken

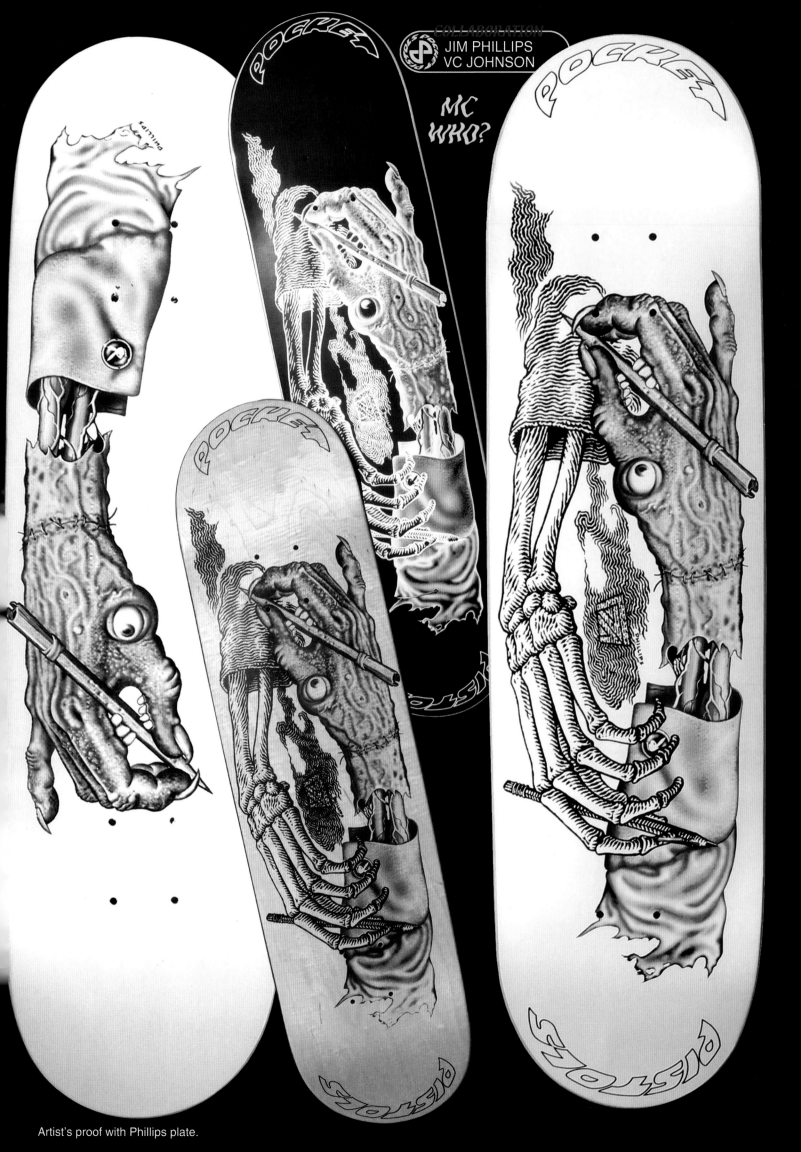

MC
WHO?

Artist's proof with Phillips plate.

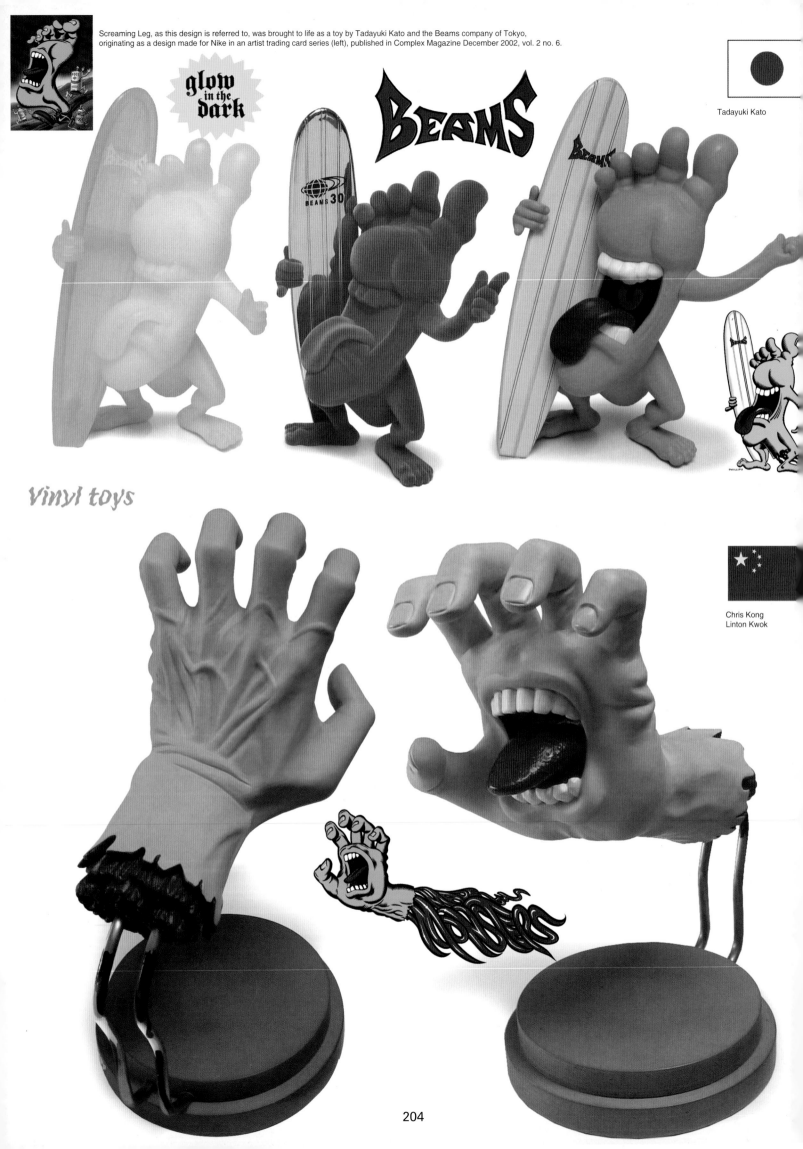

Screaming Leg, as this design is referred to, was brought to life as a toy by Tadayuki Kato and the Beams company of Tokyo, originating as a design made for Nike in an artist trading card series (left), published in Complex Magazine December 2002, vol. 2 no. 6.

glow in the dark

BEAMS

BEAMS 30

BEAMS

Tadayuki Kato

vinyl toys

Chris Kong
Linton Kwok

204

Laser art
Luca Ionescu
Collector's series

REFILL

MAGAZINE

01/30

www.refillseven.co

PHILLIPS

INDEX